EMBATTLED EDITOR

The Life of Samuel Bowles

Stephen G. Weisner

UNIVERSITY
PRESS OF
AMERICA

LANHAM • NEW YORK • LONDON

Library of Congress Cataloging-in-Publication Data

Weisner, Stephen G., 1949-
  Embattled editor.

  "Co-published by arrangement with the Institute
for Massachusetts Studies"—T.p. verso.
  Revision of the author's thesis (Ph.D., University
of Massachusetts)
  Bibliography: p.
  Includes index.
  1. Bowles, Samuel, 1826-1878. 2. Journalists—
United States—Biography. 3. Springfield republican
(Springfield, Mass. : 1855) I. Westfield State
College. Institute for Massachusetts Studies.
II. Title.
PN4874.B63W4 1986   070.4'1'0924 [B]   86-16144
  ISBN 0-8191-5603-5 (alk. paper)
  ISBN 0-8191-5604-3 (pbk. : alk. paper)

For my father, Harold Weisner 1915-1984

CONTENTS

ACKNOWLEDGMENTS

I would like to thank Springfield Mayor Richard E. Neal for providing office space to write this biography. Tim Rabbitt and Dave Bissaillon helped me "set up shop" and feel comfortable in the new surroundings.

Without a sabbatical, *Embattled Editor* might not have been written. I am grateful to Springfield Technical Community College's President, Andrew M. Scibelli, and Executive Vice-President John H. Dunn, both of whom provided support.

Librarians around the country were most helpful. I appreciated the patience and assistance of the gentlemen in the manuscripts room at the Library of Congress. Special thanks go to Arline Morton, Ed Lonergan, and Joe Carvalho at the Local History Room of the Springfield City Library. Ed and Joe lugged thirty-four years of *Springfield Republicans* from the basement and never complained about the thick dust atop each volume, nor asked me to pay their cleaning bills.

Maria Patenaude, Christine Royland, and Andrea Neary helped with secretarial chores. Carol Meuse deserves a special accolade for her typing and her uncanny ability to make sense out of my "scribbling." John Basile kindly gave me his "Bowles memento." Francis O'Leary generously shared his research on the Bowles' family genealogy.

I would like to thank my dissertation committee members, Leonard Richards, Gerald McFarland, Richard Noland, and especially Chairman Stephen B. Oates, whose faith in me will always be greatly appreciated.

I would also like to express my thanks and appreciation to Dr. Martin Kaufman, director of the Institute for Massachusetts Studies of Westfield State College. Dr. Kaufman not only read the entire manuscript, but he offered numerous suggestions which helped to improve the readability of the book. I am indebted to the staff of the Institute for Mass. Studies, Dr. Kaufman, Dr. John W. Ifkovic, and Dr. Michael F. Konig, for assuring publication of this study.

A heartfelt thanks is given to my wife, Jane Eastwood Weisner, for her constant encouragement and support and to my daughter, Sarah, just for being "the little wonder." Finally, my deepest appreciation to my mother, Anne, and sister Linda Levine. Their care and guidance has helped sustain me through the years.

INTRODUCTION

More than one hundred years ago, in 1885, George S. Merriam published a biography of Samuel Bowles. Merriam's study was more of a eulogy for a beloved friend than anything resembling an objective scholarly biography. Although the role of Samuel Bowles in local history, state history, and American history was a leading one, he lacked an objective biography. For more than a century, then, there was no scholarly biography of the person who transformed the *Springfield Republican* into a daily newspaper, and into what was acknowledged to be America's best small-city daily newspaper. The significance of Samuel Bowles was not restricted, however, to the history of journalism, or to the history of Springfield. Bowles was a founder of the Republican Party in the years prior to America's Civil War, and he was noted for his books describing travels through the American west, and through Europe. His ideas helped to shape the course of American history, and as a leading journalist many editorials originally published in the *Republican* found their way into newspapers from coast to coast, influencing national opinion in the process.

There was no doubt that a scholarly biography of Samuel Bowles was desperately needed, especially if that biography was not only based on the *Springfield Republican*, or on Bowles' correspondence and publications, but also which took into consideration the past century of historical scholarship on American political history, the history of journalism, and the history of Massachusetts and the region. The staff of the Institute for Massachusetts Studies have come to the conclusion that Stephen Weisner's biography fills that need.

The original manuscript was prepared as a doctoral dissertation at the University of Massachusetts, under the supervision of the prize-winning biographer Stephen B. Oates. Prior to publication, the dissertation was revised by the author, based on editorial suggestions provided by the staff of the Institute for Massachusetts Studies. The resulting book is, we feel, an important contribution to the literature of American political and journalistic history, as well as an important addition to the bookshelf of books related to the history of Springfield and Massachusetts.

This book represents the continuation of the work of the Institute for Massachusetts Studies, which publishes the *Historical Journal of Massachusetts*, works with Historic Deerfield and other agencies on jointly-sponsored publications, and holds annual conferences on aspects of the history and culture of the region. In 1984, the Institute joined with the New England Historic Genealogical Society in publishing Joseph Carvalho's *Black Families in Hampden County, 1650-1855*. During the same year, the Institute and the University Press of America published James A. Gelin's *Starting Over: Formation of the Jewish Community of Springfield, 1840-1905*. In 1985, the University of Massachusetts Press published a collection of essays which originated in a four-part series of symposia on "Massachusetts in the Gilded Age," which were held at the John Fitzgerald Kennedy Library, in Boston. The book, edited by Jack Tager and John W. Ifkovic, is entitled *Massachusetts in the Gilded Age: Selected Essays*. Now, the Institute for Massachusetts Studies proudly joins with the University Press of America in the publication of *Embattled Editor: The Life of Samuel Bowles*, by Stephen G. Weisner.

We would like to express our appreciation to the foundations and corporations whose financial support over the years has enabled the Institute for Massachusetts Studies not only to remain in existence, but to increase its importance in preserving the historical heritage of the state and region. Publication of this book was made possible through the generosity of those foundations and corporations whose donations were in part or whole specifically allocated toward this project. In particular, the Institute for Massachusetts Studies would like to express thanks and appreciation to

BayBank Valley Trust Company
J. Dirats and Company
Shawmut First Bank and Trust Company
Southworth Corporation
Systems Engineering and Manufacturing Company
Totsy Manufacturing Company
Western Massachusetts Electric Company
and the Westfield River Paper Company

for helping to support the work of the Institute for Massachusetts Studies. In addition, special mention must be made of

the Massachusetts Mutual Life Insurance Company
and the Frank Stanley Beveridge Foundation

both of whom provided extensive support at most crucial times in the history of the Institute, and who must be credited for their continuing and most appreciated support.

Martin Kaufman, Ph.D.
John W. Ifkovic, Ph.D.
Michael F. Konig, Ph.D.

Institute for Mass. Studies
Westfield State College

PREFACE

Samuel Bowles doesn't appear in any textbook.[1] Ninety-nine percent of my students have never heard of him, and many American history professors cannot identify him either. Yet Samuel Bowles was one of the nation's leading newspaper editors of the nineteenth century. Aside from Horace Greeley, no other editor was as well-known and influential as was the editor of *The Springfield Republican*. His thirty-three year stint at the helm of the paper—starting at the tender age of eighteen in 1844—catapulted the daily *Republican* from its provincial origins into the nation's best newspaper published outside a large city. The paper was constantly damned and praised, as was its controversial editor; but it was seldom ignored.

Bowles was a founder of the Republican Party in the turbulent 1850s.[2] He wrote travel books on the American west in the mid and late 1860s that were best sellers.[3] He was a leading advocate of "independent journalism." Heads turned as he walked through the corridors of the State House in Boston. Recognized by virtually everyone, he was feared by more than a few for what might appear in his columns the next day. No stranger in Washington, he hob-nobbed with scores of politicians and influence peddlers from throughout the country.[4]

The only biography of Bowles was published over a century ago. In two volumes and almost a thousand pages, the editor was practically deified by his friend and part-time employee, George S. Merriam.[5] The only other book containing substantive material on Bowles is Richard S. Hooker's *The Story of an Independent Newspaper*.[6] Hooker, later to be an editor of the *Republican*, was Bowles' grandson.

Bowles was a great man, with many noble qualities. But he was far from perfect. He had flaws that for perhaps obvious reasons were ignored by Merriam and Hooker. I aim in this biography to present the entire picture, warts and all, of the saint and the sinner. If Bowles were in control today, he would reprint my salutory remarks at least twice, more likely, four or five times. He always let everybody know, frequently through his newspaper, the great esteem in which he and the *Republican* were held. He would also publish the negative, but with a reply perhaps twice as long, refuting every salvo fired at him or at the paper.

Bowles' story is also that of a young America, self-assured and aggressive, but about to leave its innocence behind on the road to a cataclysmic civil war that would in many ways change the course of history.

NOTES

1. Samuel Bowles is *not* mentioned in any of the more than two dozen current American history survey texts that I have examined.

2. See Eric Foner, *Free Soil, Free Labor, Free Men* (New York: Oxford University Press, 1970).

3. Samuel Bowles, *Across the Continent: A Summer's Journey to the Rocky Mountains, the Mormons, and the Pacific States* (Springfield: Samuel Bowles and Company, 1865), *The Switzerland of America: Colorado, Its Parks and Mountains* (Springfield: Samuel Bowles and Company, 1868), *Our New West: Records of Travel Between the Mississippi River and the Pacific Ocean* (Hartford, Conn.: Hartford Publishing Company, 1869).

4. Mason Green, *Springfield, 1636-1886* (Springfield: C. A. Nichols, 1888), p. 543.

5. George S. Merriam, *The Life and Times of Samuel Bowles*, two volumes (New York: The Century Company, 1885). Although a hagiography, Merriam's work was indispensable in preparing this book. Merriam's tome was selected by Yale University librarian, James T. Babb, in 1963, as one of 1,780 titles for a reference library to "the present President and all the Presidents to come." See Scrapbooks, Springfield City Library, Local History Room, volume 37, p. 144.

6. Richard Hooker, *The Story of an Independent Newspaper* (New York: Macmillan, 1924).

CHAPTER I

THE EARLY YEARS

It was a year of great celebration—1826, the nation's golden anniversary. Americans were confident that God had blessed their land as they took heed of the biblical injunction to "hallow the fiftieth year and proclaim liberty throughout the land to all the inhabitants thereof; it shall be a jubilee unto you." Feelings of divine guidance were reinforced by the simultaneous deaths of John Adams and Thomas Jefferson on July Fourth. Adams' last words purportedly were, "Thomas Jefferson still lives."[1]

On February 9, 1826, Samuel Bowles was born, the son of Samuel Bowles of Hartford and Huldah Deming of Wethersfield, Connecticut. The Bowles family can be traced back to the original Puritan migration of the 1630s. John Bowles was an elder in the church of Roxbury in 1640 and he helped to found the Roxbury Free School. He was also a direct descendent of John Eliot, the heroic Indian Missionary and his mother's lineage can be traced to the lengendary Miles Standish.[2]

The Springfield of Bowles' birth was a small, nondescript river town of some 5,764 souls. It was bounded by a pollution-free Connecticut River on the west, Longmeadow on the south, Wilbraham on the east, and Chicopee (parts of which were originally in Springfield) on the north. "Downtown" consisted of little more than Main Street, paralleling the river north and south, and a few other intersecting roads.[3]

Springfield's historical significance lay in its being the home of a United States Armory. Although Springfield was the site of the official arsenal during the Revolutionary War, the Federal Government initially chose its sister community across the river, West Springfield, as the locale for its full-scale arms manufacturing facility. The good citizens of West Springfield staged a little "revolt," however, as they did not want the Armory upsetting their orderly, pastoral way of life. There was further concern for the virtue of the town's fair maidens, with a horde of young, single armorers living in the vicinity. Springfield, therefore, by default, gained the Armory, which would play such an important role in shaping its future history.[4]

The other major factor that would play a significant part in Springfield's growth was the railroad. Starting in 1839, when the Western Railroad entered Springfield from Worcester, some forty-five miles to the east, Springfield served as the major western New England crossroads. The town had three native sons prominent in the infant industry: George Bliss, Jr., founding president of the Western Railroad; Daniel L. Harris, the Connecticut River Railroad chief; and, most importantly, the fabulously wealthy Chester Chapin, who would head the combined Boston and Albany Railroad. All three men played active roles in the civic affairs of Springfield and were close friends of Samuel Bowles.[5]

The *Springfield Republican* was founded in 1824 by Samuel Bowles, Sr. Like all newspapers of the time, it was published on a weekly basis. The senior Bowles had been co-owner of the *Hartford Times* when he was asked by Justice Willard of Springfield to recommend a young man to come thirty miles up the valley to start a Republican newspaper in Springfield. Bowles did just that; he even accompanied the fellow to Springfield. The prospective owner, however, spurned Willard's offer. Willard then turned to Bowles, and asked if he would be interested. Bowles quickly accepted, undoubtedly happy to leave Hartford where the *Times* had accumulated a considerable debt, due in large measure to his partner's incompetence. Bowles would now be in full control of his own newspaper.[6]

He took a flatboat up the river. With him were his wife and three year-old daughter Julia, some meager articles for his new home, and, perhaps most importantly, a hand printing-press. Getting out the *Republican* would be no easy task for the elder Bowles. In its first years, all the tasks normally associated with newspaper production fell on his shoulders—publisher, editor, reporter, compositor, and pressman. "He was slow in his mental action; cautious, canny, thrifty; a prim sober man respected and trusted by everyone; undemonstrative in his family . . . but with warm and faithful affections."[7] Unlike his son, the elder Bowles rarely engendered much controversy. Several years after the elder Bowles' death, Charles Stearns, after being excoriated in the *Republican* by Samuel Bowles, Jr., wrote a letter contrasting the father and son. The father was "an able and fair minded editor, and no low personal abuse found place in the columns of the *Republican* while under his charge."[8]

Newspapers in the 1820s were a different breed from those of today. The *Republican*, a representative example, was four pages in length. The entire first and back pages typically contained all advertisements. The inner two pages were devoted to national and international news, usually of a political nature. The first issue of the *Republican* contained news from England, Greece, Russia, Mexico, and Peru. Longer items featured a biographical portrait of Lafayette and an article reprinted from the *Nantucket Inquirer* on the proposed monument to honor George Washington. A reader looking for local news would be out of luck; most likely there wouldn't be any. It was assumed that everyone knew what was going on locally.[9]

Other differences are also striking. There was, of course, no Associated Press, United Press International, or other wire services. Newspapers, therefore, got their news in large measure from other newspapers. An editor subscribed to other state, regional, national, and international newspapers and freely picked and chose the articles which he would place (often condensed) in his own newspaper. The news would obviously be somewhat less than up-to-date.[10] The biases were not kept strictly to an "editorial" section, as theoretically are contemporary newspapers, but rather infused virtually the entire contents. Indeed, before the 1830s, a typical newspaper's "raison d'être" was often to support a partisan political cause. "Objectivity" as we know it today was an alien notion. Politicians were subject to the harshest attacks, often of a personal nature that today would no doubt spawn numerous libel suits. The *Springfield Republican* was founded in such an atmosphere.[11]

The *Republican* in the title of the Springfield newspaper should not be confused with the modern political party. It was actually founded as a more liberal alternative to the Federalist newspaper then being published in town. Political parties, however, were in great flux in the 1820s; ironically, by the early 1830s, the *Republican* was firmly in the more conservative Whig camp, an ardent opponent of the new mass-based Democratic Party led by "Old Hickory," Andrew Jackson. The hero of the Battle of New Orleans easily defeated incumbent President John Quincy Adams in 1828. Jackson's victory had swift repercussions. The *Republican* had made a considerable amount of money publishing advertisements for letters remaining at the post office. Shortly after taking office, Jackson rewarded the rival *Hampden Journal* with this patronage. The *Hampden Journal* didn't support Jackson either, but it had been less strident in its opposition to him.[12]

The *Republican* of the senior Bowles was a solid and well-respected newspaper. Its successes were gradual but readily apparent. In its first issue of January 1835, the *Republican* proudly proclaimed that it had purchased its main competitor, the *Hampden Journal*. For several years afterwards, it was called the *Republican and Hampden Journal*. At about the same time, the paper was enlarged. Each page had been 14 by 19 inches, with six columns. It would become seven columns on a 17 by 21¾ inch page. Bowles agreed with many of his subscribers that the increased number of advertisements in the *Republican* was crowding out too much of the news. Politics continued to be the paper's focus, but increased attention was also given to articles on disease and related health matters.[13]

Although not reflected in the contents of the *Republican*, a revolution was going on in the newspaper business with the rise of the so-called "penny press." Prior to the 1830s, most newspapers were geared strictly to an elite audience which ended at the educated middle class. There would be no question, for example, over how to cover a sensational murder trial; it would not be covered at all. That type of story did not belong in a newspaper, argued the traditional-ists.[14] But it was precisely that type of story that helped to account for the meteoric rise of the penny press.

The *New York Sun*, the first one penny newspaper, was estab-lished in 1833. It had the highest readership total in New York City within six months of its birth. In a two year period, it tripled its circulation to fifteen thousand copies a day. Much the same story was being repeated in Boston, Philadelphia, and Baltimore.[15] The printing presses could barely keep up with the public appetite for news. In this new age of democracy, where seekers of higher office would actually have to go out and press the flesh, the people demanded and got their own newspapers as well as politicians. These great changes took place as the younger Samuel Bowles was growing up in Springfield. His *Republican* reflected both the traditionalism of his father's paper and some of the raciness of the new form.

"I was never much of a boy," he recalled. "I had very little boyhood."[16] In part that was true. Born in a modest frame house several blocks from the town center, young Sam shared his bed with Chauncey White, a young apprentice. Two other apprentices also shared a bed in the same room. Breakfast was at 6:00 a.m. sharp. By 7:00 a.m., the senior Bowles, with his apprentices, was hard at work. The boy would faithfully carry the weekly *Republican* to its subscribers and he would drive the family's cows to and from their pasture. He enjoyed gardening and would be most upset if the flowers were set upon or abused in any way. To the consternation of his father, the boy had no inclination for labor; he had no manual dexterity. If something were to be built or fixed, he would seek the assistance of his younger sister. Yet, he was a good, obedient boy. He disliked sports, and his favorite pastime was reading.[17]

The boy's formal education was modest. He attended the local schools in Springfield, making satisfactory progress in his studies. He was a diligent student, a trifle slow in absorbing material, but he usually retained most of what he learned. He enjoyed school and he had a strong desire for a college education. His headmaster, George Eaton, offered encouragement; but Bowles' hopes were dashed by his father, who thought a college education unnecessary.[18] Throughout his adult life, in the pages of his newspaper, Bowles would rationalize his lack of higher education by denigrating its value in the making of a newspaper editor. Indeed, he argued, it could be detrimental—"four years in a printing office will give a smart boy a better command of the English language than he will acquire in the same time in college . . . . The men most distinguished for mastery of the language, and for power to use it with effect," he declared, "are not college graduates . . . ."[19] In another editorial, obviously referring to his own life, Bowles exclaimed: "The college student who writes his prescribed themes with facility supposes that when he gets his degree he can fill an editorial chair with distinguished honor. If he undertakes it very likely he will find that his old schoolmate who has been educated in a printing office with a stick and rule, and the hard routine of a printer's life, makes the more popular editor and gets ahead of him in the competition for influence and wealth."[20] Bowles was not the only editor voicing such thoughts. Horace Greeley would not hire a college graduate who did not show he could overcome the "handicap" of a college education. A young man seek-

5

ing employment at the *Tribune* informed Greeley that he had just graduated from Cornell. The irascible editor replied, "I'd a damned sight rather you had graduated at a printer's case."[21] More than one observer would later wonder as to the effects a college education might have had on the maturing Bowles.[22]

His schooling over at the age of seventeen, he began the varied responsibilities of office boy at the *Republican*. Nothing in his life as yet would have given anyone the slightest hint that this tall, slim, occasionally awkward youth would one day become one of America's leading newspaper editors. His drive, ambition, and energy, let alone talent, had not surfaced.[23] Yet at some point, early in his eighteenth year, an idea took shape: to make the *Republican* a daily newspaper. The senior Bowles was taken aback by the suggestion. He was by nature a cautious man, and undertaking a daily newspaper was a monumental task not without great risk. Young Sam, however, was persistent. He pushed his idea with a determination that must have surprised, if not shocked, his doubting father. There was not a single daily newspaper in the state outside of Boston. Nothing in the make-up of the small, provincial town gave any indication that a daily newspaper could gain sufficient support. Bowles senior, nearing his fiftieth birthday and not in the best of health, was enjoying the success of his weekly. His son, however, would not let the idea die. Finally, after much soul-searching and still harboring doubts, the father gave in, telling his boy, "If you, Sam, will take the main responsibility of working and publishing it, the daily shall be started."[24] Bowles received five hundred dollars per year, as his father relinquished most of the editorial duties and concentrated on the financial side of the business. Thus the stage was set for the junior Bowles and his daily newspaper.[25]

The elder Bowles' doubts were evident in the first issue on March 27, 1844. The public was told that the daily was an "experiment" and that the newspaper had started without a single subscriber or committed long-term advertiser. The newspaper would be given from six months to a year to succeed. Springfield citizens were urged to read their own daily newspaper; "if our little daily could have one-half of what is paid in Springfield for New York and Boston papers it would ensure its support."[26] The *Republican* cost four dollars a year, payable in advance. Single copies were not generally available. Advertisers were charged $20 a year for one square daily (changed whenever wished), $5.50 for three months, $1.50 per week, and 75 cents for a single day.[27] Farm products were accepted in lieu of cash, and were taken to a local store for credit.[28]

The daily *Republican* emphasized political topics, but unlike the weekly, it did not ignore matters of local interest. That would be young Sam's beat. He would scour the community, in essence asking people, "What's new? " The *Republican* began naming visitors who were staying at the major hotels in town, and their "business."[29] He did a good deal of his work at night. The type of the newspaper, except for half a column, would be set by 9:00 p.m. Young Sam would leave his copy of local items in the wee hours of the morning, the last items added before publication.[30] Bowles then, and throughout his life, always wanted to know everything that was going on. He was not very good at keeping secrets. A critic, looking back on his life, called him, and not without reason, a "great gossip."[31]

The pages of the *Republican* were filled with a wide variety of subject matter aside from its political contents. There was practical advice—"Take to the right when you meet any person on the sidewalk, and never walk more than two abreast. Consider that others have some right to the sidewalk as well as yourself and immediate companions."[32] Readers were informed authoritatively that . . . "there were two hundred and two suicides committed in the United States last year. Of these numbers, 38 were by cutting the throat, 52 hanging, 29 shooting, 25 drowning, 22 poison, 10 jumping from a height, 6 stabbing, 6 under railroad cars. Of this number 59 were insane, 15 drunk, and 18 filled with remorse and despair."[33]

Humor was a staple of most newspapers during the period, and the *Republican* was no exception. It ran the gamut from play on words or puns, to ethnic humor and the ribald, to the "Ripley's Believe It or Not" type. "'I never catch a cold,' said a loafer—'No, you are too lazy,' was said in reply."[34] A person asked an Irishman why he wore his stockings the wrong side out. "'Bekase,' said he, 'there's a hole on the other side.'"[35] "'Why is Henry Clay like a successful lover?'—'Because he can 'come in.'"[36] "An 81-year-old lady died. A post mortem exam found that inside the woman's stomach was a fully developed female child . . . ."[37]

Young Sam threw himself into his work. There was little rest or relaxation; he never did learn how to relax. The result, in less than a year, was a physical breakdown. *Republican* readers were informed that he "has gone South to spend the winter at the advice of a physician for the single object of recovering his health." Since his arrival in New Orleans, the paper added, he was feeling better.[38] Yet his recovery was likely slowed by his main activity there, writing. The nineteen year old convalescent wrote a series of fifteen letters back to the *Republican*, dealing with a wide variety of topics that he thought would interest his readers.[39]

The articles were written in a straightforward, easy-to-read style. They were mostly descriptive, with only fragments of analysis. He noted the warm weather he was enjoying in contrast to his freezing brethren, and he was taken by the beauty of the St. Charles Hotel. He was less pleased by the expensive rates—a princely $2 to $3 a day.[40] On more substantive matters, he described the commercial activities at the busy port of New Orleans and the proceedings in the Louisiana legislature concerning the Texas annexation question.[41] Perhaps his best letter was a detailed and careful account of the inner workings of the sugar business—from soil, to production, to marketing.[42]

Feeling better—his health could never be described as vibrant—he returned to New England in the spring of 1845. As usual, he spared no energy returning to work. Capturing his immediate attention was a controversy at the town's major employer, the United States Armory. Shortly before his death, reminiscing with a friend, he was asked if there was any one thing in his life that started him on his road to success. Bowles said there was. "Soon after I took hold of the paper there was a quarrel about the management of the Armory. The men who differed with my father made it a personal matter against him, and tried to break down his business by starting an opposition paper. That roused my ire, and I determined that we would not be beaten."[43]

The dispute at the Armory centered around the installation of a Major James W. Ripley as the new superintendent. Ripley was a military man, not a civilian, as had been the tradition at the Armory. Ripley cracked the whip, as reports had reached Washington concerning lack of discipline and low productivity. Some workers, for example, openly drank strong liquors on the job. Others played cards during the work day. The *Republican* argued, however, that the change to military command was illegal and that the superintendent should be a civilian experienced in the manufacturing of arms. The problem with lax workers, it thought, was exaggerated. The *Republican* inveighed against Ripley's despotic demeanor and his wholesale firing of veteran armorers. The debate dragged on for years. At one point, formal charges were drawn against Ripley and an investigation was held at the Capitol, but he was acquitted of all charges. In later years, the *Republican* praised Ripley's character and leadership capabilities.[44]

Competition from the *Springfield Gazette* improved the *Republican*. The *Republican* was enlarged to five pages with a new and cleaner look. Readers were informed that the news would be received even faster because of the telegraph.[45] It began reporting comprehensive election returns for which it achieved later renown.[46] By the spring of 1846, its daily circulation had increased to over four hundred.[47] Rapidly losing money, the owner of the *Gazette* was willing to sell the paper, and on July 1, 1848, the *Republican* announced that it had purchased the *Gazette* and that it would unite its subscription lists with those of the daily and weekly *Republican*.[48] The cost was approximately $2,250.00 which included printing materials. The daily *Republican* gained some two hundred new subscribers and the weekly gained about six hundred. There would be no serious challenge to the paper's supremacy in Springfield for almost another generation.

The newspaper's local coverage, already a popular feature in the town, expanded with the addition of a semi-regular column entitled "LIFE IN SPRINGFIELD."[49] The column, written by Samuel Bowles, Jr., was especially intended for distant subscribers to inform them of the news they may have missed. The feature was written in an "easy slouching style," and in letter form. Much of what he wrote reflected the boosterism of the times: "Springfield is a great place . . . of beauty and vigor . . . [with] prosperous manufacturers, elegant stores and unrivaled hotels."[50] Future columns dealt with gaslights, a prominent minister's fortieth anniversary sermon,[51] new buildings, and local entertainment.[52]

Bowles also started the practice of covering college commencements in western Massachusetts. College commencements in mid-nineteenth century America were important events, and ceremonies often lasted an entire week. The first one which he attended as a reporter was at Amherst College, where he later became a trustee. He faithfully reported the speech of the commencement speaker, James

S. Thayer of New York City, whose topic was the "Commercial Spirit."[53] This was probably Bowles' first trip to Amherst, but he returned often in later years, as he became close to several members of the Dickinson family.

While his father was busy in the counting room and Samuel, Jr. was editing the daily and scurrying around town for local news, two men were writing political editorials on an ad hoc basis, William B. Calhoun and George Ashmun. Calhoun had started writing editorials for the *Republican* back in the 1820s and continued off and on until 1847. His trenchant analysis and brilliant exposition added to the newspaper's early reputation. Calhoun's experience was most impressive: member of the Massachusetts House of Representatives, Speaker of the House, State Senator and Senate President, Mayor of Springfield, and United States Congressman. He was, as Bowles would later write in his obituary, "THE PUBLIC MAN" of Springfield. There is little doubt that Bowles tried to emulate his "pure . . . popular and enticing style."[54]

Ashmun, like Calhoun a Massachusetts House and Senate member and a Congressman, also profoundly influenced Bowles. He would later say that Ashmun was the only man who ever dominated him. Ashmun, who lived a stone's throw from Bowles, helped the boy learn the social graces. Bowles learned from Ashmun how to draw out the best in people, how to feel at ease, and he gained confidence in his social relationships. Bowles recalled that Ashmun, "At his own or friend's dinner table was almost incomparably felicitious. He had a thought and word for everybody at the table, men, women, or child, and it fitted exactly to the level of each life." At a dinner in Springfield for William M. Thackeray, Bowles remembered that Ashmun "led in the feast of good things, skillfully avoiding all possible shoals, smoothing the ruffling of any feathers that might come from any trans-atlantic prejudices or thoughtless remark." Bowles further recalled that one guest dubbed Ashmun, "The most brilliant table-talker of America."[55]

It wasn't all toil for the young editor. In early September 1848, he managed to take some time off. He journeyed several hundred miles west to Geneva, New York, to marry Mary Sanford Dwight Schermerhorn. Mary was the granddaughter of James S. Dwight, Springfield's leading merchant of the early nineteenth century and most likely the town's wealthiest man. It was said that "The

Dwights ruled Springfield."[56] Mary also had blood ties to the dynastic Van Rensselaer family of New York.[57] Both the twenty-three year old bride and twenty-four year old groom had been classmates at Mr. Eaton's school in Springfield. During the school year, Mary had lived with her uncle, one of many relatives she had in town. There was no time for a honeymoon; married on a Wednesday, he was back to the office three days later.[58] On the whole, it would be a strong marriage. She endured his frequent absences, while suffering from health problems and ten mostly difficult pregnancies. Her loyalty to him and jealousy cannot be doubted, nor his genuine concern and affection for her. Once asked to account for his success, he replied to a young associate, "I married early . . . ."[59]

The newlyweds lived in the Bowles' home, and the father continued to pay his son a $500 salary. His financial picture changed dramatically, however, when his wife inherited $10,000. Bowles promptly bought some prime real estate—the block to which the *Republican* had recently moved. His father in turn gave his namesake one-half ownership of the newspaper.[60] Through his wife, then, he attained financial security.

1848 was a significant year for the United States. The Mexican War was over; America had gained a "great victory" over its impoverished, southern neighbor. That same year, the slavery issue dominated Congress as the lawmakers vigorously debated the fate of the new lands, the spoils of war, now in America's control. Would they be slave territory or free?[61] And, in the midst of the often bitter political struggle, the cry of gold would shortly echo across the land, as thousands risked their lives by land or sea for the chance at quick riches in California.[62] It was during the late 1840s that Bowles gradually began to shift his focus from local concerns to national issues. It was in the presidential election of 1848 that his voice began to be heard loud and clear.

NOTES

1. James MacGregor Burns, *The Vineyard of Liberty* (New York: Vintage, 1983), pp. 270-273.

2. Genealogical and Historical Notes of the Bowles Family, 1851.

3. *Springfield Chronology Nineteenth Century*, a thin pamphlet without an author or page numbers, in Local History Room, Springfield Public Library.

4. Green, p. 354, and Michael Frisch, *Town Into City: Springfield, Massachusetts and the Meaning of Community, 1840-1880* (Cambridge: Harvard University Press, 1972), p. 16.

5. Frisch, p. 19.

6. Hooker, p. 4.

7. Merriam, I:3-4.

8. Charles Stearns to Samuel Bowles, August 1854 in Samuel Bowles folder, Local History Room, Springfield Public Library.

9. *Springfield Republican* (Hereafter abbreviated as *S.R.*, all references in this study will be to the daily paper), March 27, 1844; Hooker, p. 16.

10. Michael Schudson, *Discovering the News: A Social History of American Newspapers* (New York: Basic Books, 1978), p. 14.

11. John C. Miller, *The Federalist Era* (New York: Harper and Row, 1960), pp. 89-93.

12. Hooker, pp. 22-24; Thomas Bailey, *The American Pageant* (Lexington: D. C. Heath, Seventh Edition, 1983), p. 223.

13. Ibid., p. 30.

14. Schudson, p. 23.

15. Williard Bleyer, *Main Currents in the History of American Journalism* (Boston: Houghton Mifflin, 1927), p. 166.

16. Merriam, I:19.

17. Ibid., p. 15; Hooker, pp. 36-37.

18. Ibid., p. 16.

19. *S.R.*, August 20, 1858, p. 2, col. I. See also July 28, 1860.

20. Ibid., April 12, 1859, p. 2, col. I.

21. Schudson, p. 68.

22. Henry M. Whitney, *New England and Yale Review*, February 1886, pp. 97-107.

23. Washington Gladden, *Dial*, February 1886, p. 21.

24. Merriam, I:21.

25. *Monthly Newsletter*, City Library, January 1889, p. 2.

26. *S.R.*, March 27, 1844, p. 2, col. I. Over one hundred forty years later the problem remains. Springfield citizens are still buying those New York and Boston newspapers!

27. Ibid., p. 1, col. I.

28. Hooker, p. 39.

29. *S.R.*, May 7, 1844. This column was not too popular, lasting about a month.

30. Hooker, p. 43.

31. *The Nation*, XLI:553. No author is given although in the *Dictionary of American Biography* Allen Nevins thinks the author was Wendell Phillips Garrison.

32. *S.R.*, April 13, 1844, p. 2, col. I.

33. Ibid., May 5, 1847, p. 3, col. I.

34. Ibid., May 13, 1844.

35. Ibid., June 12, 1844.

36. Ibid., June 12, 1844.

37. Ibid., November 14, 1850, p. 2, col. III.

38. Ibid., January 15, 1845, p. 2, col. III.

39. Hooker, p. 42.

40. *S.R.*. January 15, 1845, p. 2, col. III.

41. Ibid., January 30, 1845, p. 2, col. I.

42. Ibid., February 20, 1845, p. 2, col. I.

43. Merriam, I:23.

44. Hooker, pp. 44-45; *S.R.*, March 17, 1870; Derwent S. Whittlesey, *The Springfield Armory* (Ph.D. dissertation, University of Chicago, 1920), chapter six.

45. *S.R.*, April 1, 1846, p. 2, col. II.

46. Merriam, I:24.

47. *S.R.*, April 10, 1846, p. 2, col. III.

48. Ibid., July 1, 1848, p. 2, col. I.

49. Hooker, p. 46.

50. *S.R.*, January 16, 1849, p. 2, col. I.

51. Ibid., February 1, 1849, p. 2, col. I.

52. Ibid., February 21, 1849, p. 2, col. III.

53. Ibid., August 10, 1849, p. 2, col. III.

54. Ibid., November 9, 1865; Merriam, I:36-37.

55. Hooker, p. 49; Merriam, I:43.

56. Green, p. 385.

57. *Time and the Our*, January 21, 1899, vol. IX, number seven.

58. Merriam, I:56.

59. Hooker, p. 56.

60. Frank Bauer, *At the Crossroads: Springfield, Massachusetts 1636-1975* (Springfield: Bicentennial Committee of Springfield, 1975), p. 44.

61. Otis Singletary, *The Mexican War* (Chicago: University of Chicago Press, 1960).

62. J. S. Holliday, *The World Rushed In: The California Gold Rush Experience* (New York: Simon and Schuster, Touchstone Edition, 1983).

CHAPTER II

ENTERING THE POLITICAL ARENA

The presidential election of 1848 was a heated contest. Zachary Taylor, "Old Rough and Ready," a victorious general in the Mexican War, was nominated by the Whigs. The Democratic standard-bearer was Senator Lewis Cass of Michigan, an aging party warhorse. The Free Soil Party, a renegade group of disenchanted Whigs and Democrats, ran former president Martin Van Buren. The campaign's major issue was slavery—or more precisely—the question of slave expansion into the west. The Free Soilers were firm against the expansion of slavery. Cass favored "popular sovereignty," that is, letting the people of each territory decide for themselves whether slaves would be admitted or excluded. What Taylor stood for was pretty much a secret; although he was a slave-owner, he did not say much and the Whigs cynically refused to publish a platform.[1]

Into the political fray stepped the young Samuel Bowles. "For a good while," Chauncey White recalled, "he didn't do much political writing. But one evening in a presidential campaign—it was in the Taylor year—he had been out to report a speech and he came in tearing mad and sat down and wrote a reply to it . . . that was about the beginning of Mr. Bowles' political writing."[2] White was referring to an early June editorial in the *Springfield Republican*. Free Soiler Joshua Giddings had come to Springfield seeking support for his new party, but Bowles was incredulous. How, he wondered, could these Free Soilers be touting Martin Van Buren. After all, during his whole political life Van Buren had been the "most abject tool of the slave power." He reminded his readers that Van Buren's tenure as chief executive was a dismal failure, replete with a devastating depression, and that Van Buren richly deserved his nickname "Martin Van Ruin." Despite his opposition to Van Buren, Bowles assured his subscribers that he was strongly against the expansion of slavery, "Our efforts are pledged to this end," he declared. Although Taylor was a Louisiana slaveholder, Bowles, along with many of the Whigs, held to

15

the impression that Taylor was on his side.[3] Bowles was practically compelled to support Taylor, as that summer he was appointed Secretary of the Springfield Whigs.[4] Taylor won—although by a surprisingly narrow margin—and the *Republican* rejoiced. Bowles, exhausted but exhilarated, relished his role in the political battle.

After Taylor's election, the rhetoric in the halls of Congress reached fever pitch. The seeds of disunion were planted in the rancorous political debate. First, sixty-three ballots were needed to elect a new Speaker of the House. Then, an agreement was finally reached on the controversial issue of slavery—the Compromise of 1850. Introduced by Henry Clay, the Compromise was engineered into law by the "Little Giant," Stephen Douglas. This measure, among other things, brought California into the Union as a free state and ended the slave trade, but not slavery, in the nation's capital. These provisions largely pleased northerners. Southerners were favored with a newly-toughened Fugitive Slave law, which made it easier for Southerners to regain their runaway slaves. Under the new law, a slaveholder claimed a fugitive by petitioning a federal commissioner, who could order the slave's return. Northerners were incensed that the law forced private citizens and local government officials to aid federal authorities in enforcing this law.[5]

Many New Englanders and particularly Bay Staters were outraged by Daniel Webster's role in the Congressional drama. His "Seventh of March" speech in the Senate urged compromise, concessions, and reasonableness on all sides. How, anti-slavery northerners wondered, could he support any bill that included the accursed Fugitive Slave Act? The poet Whittier responded in verse:

> So fallen, so lost, the light withdrawn
> Which once he wore
> The Glory from his gray hairs gone
> For evermore![6]

Bowles' support of Webster's speech was restrained. In a special edition, he praised its patriotic tenor, but ruefully wished "that it had been more than it is."[7] Bowles found himself in a ticklish situation. George Ashmun, the contributing columnist whom he idolized, was one of Webster's closest friends.

Early in the following year, 1851, George Thompson, the outspoken English abolitionist, visited Springfield. His visit was less than pleasant. The majority of northerners in the ante-bellum period were anti-slavery as well as anti-abolitionist. A typical northerner did not like slavery and would have preferred its demise. But he also acknowledged the constitutional right of southerners to own slaves. At this time, he was certainly not willing to risk sectional strife or disunion to aid those in bondage. Abolitionists were perceived as radicals and extremists. William Lloyd Garrison had written that the United States Constitution, that most revered of documents, was a "Covenant with Death and an agreement with Hell . . . and [it] should be immediately annulled."[8]

When Thompson had first toured America in the summer of 1835, he met stiff opposition. He faced loud hecklers and was an easy target of ardent egg-throwers.[9] Threats on his life prompted an earlier-than-anticipated return to England.[10] Back in America some fifteen years later, he found that anti-abolitionist fever had dissipated, largely a result of the Fugitive Slave Act. Unlike his earlier trip, he was treated politely. There was, however, one notable exception: Springfield, Massachusetts. The day before he arrived in town, his effigy hung along with that of "John Bull," England's "Uncle Sam." Inflammatory handbills were distributed around town, urging the people of Springfield, and especially the Irish, to "drive this miscreant from our soil . . . and give this British Emissary a reception that will teach a new lesson to English Statesmen."[11]

The February 17th *Republican* was largely devoted to Thompson's impending visit. Bowles wrote that William Lloyd Garrison and Wendell Phillips would accompany the Englishman to Springfield. In thunderous tones, Bowles declared that these men would be "denouncing the American Constitution, libeling the Christian Church, and abusing the greatest and best men, living and dead, that have ever impressed their names upon our country's history." It would be, said the editor, "a scene of pitiful fanaticism, blind perversion of truth, and such handling of sacred things as shall wound the moral sense like the naked blow of blasphemy."[12] A month earlier, Bowles had castigated Thompson for his remarks made in Plymouth about Daniel Webster. When Thompson lamented the fact that he could not visit Mammouth Cave for fear of violence, Bowles replied that he not only should have been allowed to visit, but forced to stay there![13]

Meanwhile, the Springfield selectmen met in emergency session. They formed a committee that met Thompson upon his arrival in Springfield, and they warned him of the ill-feeling in town that could possibly result in violence to him and his cohorts. Thompson listened politely and declared that he had no intention of leaving. The selectmen promptly passed a resolution which said in part that they, as "representatives of the town of Springfield, are not responsible for any injuries or damage that may take place." That night, a mob of some two hundred men and boys gathered outside Thompson's hotel room. The cacophony of noise, replete with firecrackers, drums, fifes, and bells echoed across the downtown streets. In addition, a variety of objects from eggs and stones to "missiles" struck his hotel window. Finally, shortly before dawn, the mob dispersed.[14]

That morning, the sparsely attended abolitionist meeting was held in Dwight Hall. Sheriff Caleb Rice was there to prevent any possible conflict. Thompson lashed out at his opposition, accusing the selectmen of attempting to deny his freedom of speech and passionately refuting the attack on his character. After a lunch break, the abolitionists reconvened at the African Church on Sanford Street. Thompson's target was the man who, he was certain, had instigated the mob the night before, and who had printed the inflammatory handbill, Samuel Bowles. The Englishman called Bowles "a venal scribbler, a bread and butter patriot, a crocodile luminary of the *Republican*." That evening, in reaction to criticism of their town and its newspaper, hundreds gathered once again to "serenade" the acerbic abolitionist. The mob was louder and more menacing than it had been the first night. They cheered lustily as Thompson once again was burned in effigy. Thompson did have his supporters, however. After the mob left, a group of Negroes demonstrated their appreciation by singing and cheering. The next day, Thompson and his entourage left town for his next speaking engagement. At the railroad station, he was the target of uncomplimentary shouting and rotten eggs.

Bowles' behavior in the Thompson episode was shameful. Instead of defending the right of free speech, he gave tacit approval to mob rule. In the matter of the Fugitive Slave Act, he condemned those who sought to disrupt the deportation of runaway slaves. Speaking from a legalistic rather than moral perspective, "Our simple duty," he wrote, "is . . . to offer no resistance to the recapture of fugitive slaves." "If we do," he exclaimed, "our Constitution is worthless . . . ."[16]

18

Later that year, personal tragedy struck the *Republican.* Bowles' sister, Mrs. Julia Foote, lost a baby in childbirth, and ten days later, she died. Within the same month, his fifty-four year-old father passed away. The paper reported that "His fatal disease was dysentery, aggravated by a chronic bowel difficulty. He had been sick two weeks, and, though suffering painfully throughout, was conscious to the last moment."[17] Now that his father was dead, Bowles no longer added "Jr." to his signed columns.

The business side of the paper increased Bowles' list of responsibilities. He worked as hard as ever, but the burden was overwhelming. As the days progressed, he grew weaker. His head throbbed unmercifully, and for a time, he feared he was going blind. An attack of inflammatory rheumatism added to his physical woes. Taking the advice of family, he traveled to New York City for medical treatment. While there, he stayed at the Brooklyn home of his sister, Mrs. Henry Alexander.[18] He wrote a short note published in his newspaper thanking his friends for their concern and telling them that he "hoped to get around when the weather does."[19]

He returned home in the summer, eager to get back to work. "Home," however, was now a new two-story structure on Maple Street, a street with a commanding view of the river, the surrounding hills, and the adjoining downtown section. Bowles was now able to literally keep an eye on his beloved Springfield. The move to Maple Street was plotted by his wife and mother during his New York convalescence, and he was delighted.[20]

Meanwhile, a deceptive calm had settled over the political landscape. Most Americans accepted—albeit some grudgingly—the basic terms of the Compromise of 1850. Many people foolishly believed that the law had actually resolved the slavery issue once and for all. But in 1854, the calm became a storm, when Stephen Douglas of Illinois introduced an act in the Senate calling for the formation of two new territorial governments for Kansas and Nebraska in the unorganized area north of the 36° 30' line. This slave status would be determined by popular sovereignty. Whatever his motivation, the proposed legislation heated the slave issue. Douglas was dead wrong when he declared "that this measure will be as popular at the North as at the South."[21]

The Kansas-Nebraska Act repealed the Missouri Compromise of 1820, which had prohibited slavery in the Louisiana Territory north of the 36° 30' line. Slavery, under Douglas' act, was now possible there. Douglas thought he could gain favor with both sections—with southerners pleased at the prospect of slave expansion and with northerners knowing that the territory, by virtue of climate and topography, was unsuited for slavery. It was an incredible miscalculation, and the northern reaction was swift. Bowles' *Springfield Republican* reflected the prevailing sentiment in the north: "It is a monstrous proposition. It is a huge stride backwards . . . the South and its allies have broken the peace of the country. They make fresh and monstrous demands. These demands . . . will widen and deepen the anti-slavery feeling of the country as no other conceivable proposition could." [22]

At about the same time that "Kansas-Nebraska" was enacted into law, a black man from Virginia, Anthony Burns, was arrested in Boston as a fugitive slave. C. G. Loring, United States Commissioner and Massachusetts Probate Judge, issued a warrant for his return to slavery. Bostonians seethed with indignation, and rumors of planned violence spread through the port city. An attempt was made to rescue the prisoner, but it failed and Burns was sent back into bondage. He left Boston having been protected by a hundred special deputies of the United States Marshall, a contingent of marines, a thousand militia, and the entire local police force. [23]

Three years earlier, Bowles supported Springfield's anti-abolitionist mob and urged his readers to support the statute. The Kansas-Nebraska Act had changed his thinking. "The world now understands . . . that the interest cherished most warmly by the American government is property in human flesh . . . slavery rules today . . . shall it always do this? Aye! So long as we fraternize politically with men who have made us their slave-catchers, and use our halls of justice for slave pens." [24] In 1855, a call was issued for Judge Loring's impeachment, and Bowles approved. Earlier, he editorialized that Loring was doing his duty, obeying the law of the land. Now he propounded the notion of a higher law, saying "we would refuse to obey or execute some laws and the Fugitive Slave Law is one of them . . . ." Bowles endorsed Coleridge's adage that "the man who squares his conscience by the law was a common synonym for a wretch without any conscience at all." [25]

20

Whatever political consensus had existed prior to 1854 collapsed as a result of Kansas-Nebraska. The Democratic Party now was increasingly dominated by its southern wing. Although Franklin Pierce, a New Hampshire native, was president, he was considered a "dough face," a northern man with southern principles. Meanwhile, the Whig party was torn apart by its rival "cotton" and "conscience" factions, and it was a dying party. Into this vacuum burst a new movement and a new party, the "Know-Nothings." The Know-Nothings were so called because when asked about their "secret" organization, members replied, "I know nothing." The party was a response to the turmoil and confusion of the times. Members feared the immigration—largely Irish and Roman Catholic—that, according to its adherents, was a threat to the American way of life. Its instant success stunned the political establishment. In Massachusetts, for example, the party garnered sixty-three percent of the vote and swept candidates into office at every level of government. The governor, the entire congressional delegation, and all forty state senators bore the Know-Nothing label.[26]

Bowles opposed the new party at the outset. He found it "reprehensible" and objected to its tendency to "keep alive prejudices."[27] Bowles strongly attacked its successful candidate for governor, Henry Gardner. Gardner responded with several personal letters to the editor, complaining about his unfair attacks and "torturous course."[28] Bowles' analysis of the election was right on target. After the Know-Nothing sweep, he wrote: "The result of Monday's voting means that people were out of humor with the old political organizations, and desired to extinguish them, break down the differences, unite and redivide . . . . The people, disappointed and vexed, seized on Know-Nothingism as an instrument for breaking to pieces the old parties." Bowles was especially saddened that some good men, like western Massachusetts Congressman Edward Dickinson of Amherst, were spurned by the voters.[29]

Bowles soon earned the party's enmity. In June of 1855, the Know-Nothings held a meeting of their National Council in Philadelphia. All members swore an oath of secrecy; everything said at the meeting was to be held in the strictest confidence. But something went wrong! Each day the meeting's contents were published, virtually verbatim, in not just one newspaper, but three—the *New York Tribune*, the *Boston Atlas*, and the *Springfield Republican*. The articles were similar in tone and content, with good reason: all three accounts were written by the same man, Samuel Bowles. Bowles got his information from "indirect and unusual avenues."[30] His source was actually the Massachusetts delegation and, in particular, Senator Henry Wilson who represented the anti-slavery wing of the party. The Know-Nothings had adopted a blatantly pro-southern platform. Wilson and his cohorts, therefore, felt justified in disclosing the Council's business. At session's end, a meeting was held by Wilson, Bowles, and Whig stalwart Ezra Lincoln. They agreed on one basic point—that the time was ripe for a united Republican movement in Massachusetts.[31]

This would be no easy task. Two hands were needed to count the myriad parties, factions, and movements around the country. Besides the familiar Democrats and Whigs, Know-Nothings and Free Soilers, there were "Temperance Men, Rum Democrats, Silver Gray Whigs, Hindoos, Hard Shell Democrats, Soft Shells, and Half Shells."[32] Bowles publicly reiterated his belief that the time had come for the formation of a new party. He urged a state convention to inaugurate "a party of freedom."[33] Almost all the press, he added—the old Whig press, the Free-Soil, and most of the independent journals—were supporting the idea of a new party.[34] After considerable delay, a meeting took place at the United States Hotel in Boston, with Bowles as chairman. A committee of prominent figures, including Charles Francis Adams, Richard Henry Dana Jr., George Boutwell, and Henry L. Dawes, was formed for the purpose of organizing a state convention. They called for a simultaneous mass and delegate convention to meet in Worcester on September 20, 1855.[35]

That gathering was a raucous one. Most of those in attendance agreed that "the repeal of the Missouri Compromise renders every inch of the national domain a battleground between freedom and slavery. It makes the admission of every new state a conflict between freedom and slavery."[36] But the nomination for governor was fractious. By the narrowest of margins, incumbent Governor Gardner lost the Republican nomination to the old Whig, Julius Rockwell. The moribund Whigs nominated Samuel Valley, the Democrats' choice was E. D. Beach, and the Know-Nothings re-nominated Gardner. Gardner won, but it was more a personal triumph than a party victory, as Know-Nothing fever was rapidly ebbing. The political picture remained muddled. The Republican Party, however, gained a toehold in the state, although it lagged behind the progress that Republicans were making in other states, especially in the mid-west.[37]

The Republican party surged rapidly the next year in Massachusetts and everywhere above the Mason-Dixon line. Its growth was spawned by the increasingly heated rhetoric and violence that permeated the troubled nation. Massachusetts' own Senator Charles Sumner, for example, after unleashing an admittedly vituperative speech against South Carolina's Senator Andrew P. Butler, was attacked and knocked senseless on the Senate floor. The culprit, armed with a heavy wooden cane, was Butler's nephew, Congressman Preston Brooks, also of South Carolina. The unremorseful ruffian recalled, "I gave him about thirty first rate stripes. Towards the last he bellowed like a calf. I wore my cane out completely but saved the head which is gold."[38] While Brooks was being praised in Dixie, Bowles expressed the prevailing northern outrage and used the incident to promote the Republican Party. "There is no denying the humiliating fact that this country is under the reign of ruffianism . . . . Free speech . . . may only be indulged in at the cost of a beaten head . . . . Old party names must be forgotten, old party ties surrendered, organizations based upon secondary issues abandoned, [and] momentary self-interest sacrificed to the country and its welfare . . . ."[39]

That year, 1856, Bowles wrote dispatches from all three political convention sites. In Philadelphia, he reported openly on the proceedings of the Know-Nothing party, which had lifted its veil of secrecy. Former president Millard Fillmore was nominated on a basically pro-slavery platform. Massachusetts' members then bolted the meeting.[40] The Democrats met in the "Queen City of the West," Cincinnati, and nominated another doughface, James Buchanan of Pennsylvania. Buchanan was Ambassador to England and, thus was unsullied by the slave issue. Bowles argued forcefully that the Democrats were playing games with the people. He noted that Buchanan had "contrived to keep himself disassociated from the acts which have made that of Franklin Pierce execrable . . . ."[41] He believed the resolutions passed by the Democrats were a pack of lies, and he insisted that the Democrats were really putting slavery and freedom on the same plane.[42]

The weary Bowles returned to Philadelphia that summer to attend the first national Republican convention. Nominated on the first ballot was dashing, forty-three year-old John C. Fremont. Fremont, the "Pathfinder," was well-known for his exploration of California and his military successes. The new Republican Party had followed the old pragmatic Whig tradition in nominating its most

23

attractive candidate, not its most qualified.[43] Bowles knew it was the anti-slavery cause, not the man, that was of paramount importance. In an uncharacteristically long sentence, he wrote, "Pure as is the life of Colonel Fremont, spotless as his reputation, noble as are his traits of character, high as are his accomplishments, and devotedly as the people love him, his name in any public assembly of Republicans awakens no responses like those which greet the annunciation of the sentiments which he represents."[44]

Fremont lost the election that November, but Bowles was neither surprised nor discouraged. He was confident that the Republican Party would one day prevail. The Whigs were dying, and the Democrats represented the ignorant masses and timid aristocrats. These groups were on the decline. The Republican Party, on the other hand, represented "those who work with their hands, who live and act independently, who hold the stakes of home and family, of farm and workshop, of education and freedom."[45] The Republican Party, thought Bowles, was destined to rule.

Two days after Buchanan was inaugurated, the Supreme Court handed down the historic Dred Scott decision. Basically, it was a simple case. Dred Scott was the slave of Dr. John Emerson of St. Louis. Emerson joined the army as a surgeon and was assigned to duty at Rock Island, Illinois. Later, he was transferred to Fort Snelling in the Wisconsin territory. He then returned to his native Missouri. Scott, his body servant and slave, accompanied him on all his travels. After Emerson's death in 1846, Scott, with the aid of abolitionist lawyers, brought suit in the Missouri courts. Scott's lawyers argued that residence in Illinois, where slavery was outlawed under the old Northwest Ordinance of 1787, and in the Wisconsin Territory, where it was barred by the Missouri Compromise, had made him a free man. After many years of litigation, the case finally reached the Supreme Court, and the decision rocked the foundations of the nation. The high court ruled that the Missouri Compromise was unconstitutional. Neither Congress nor, presumably, any territorial government could exclude slavery from public lands. In essence, slavery was national, freedom sectional. Northerners were shocked; southerners rejoiced. Sectional distrust heightened.[46]

Once again, Bowles and his *Republican* echoed mainstream northern opinion. The justices could have issued a narrow, technical decision, but they did not. The Supreme Court was a tool of the south, of southern Democrats, and the slave interest. Bowles predicted that the decision "would widen and deepen, rather than allay, agitations."[47] Later, he wrote that the ruling was "just as binding as if it was uttered by a southern debating club, and no more."[48] Attitudes hardened. Northerners believed that a "slave power conspiracy" had gained control of the nation, determined to push slavery across the land, perhaps even beyond the nation's border. On the other hand, southerners were convinced that the hidden agenda of the north and its Republican Party was the total eradication of slavery, not just stopping its expansion. Both attitudes were reinforced by the actions of a one-time Springfield resident, John Brown.

Brown had moved to Springfield in 1846, setting up a wool business called Perkins and Brown. Perkins, an affluent Ohio businessman, provided the financial backing. Brown sorted wool and sold it by grades, charging a commission of two cents per pound. The venture failed and Brown left Springfield. In 1851, however, he returned and organized the "Springfield Gileadites," a group dedicated to resisting the capture of fugitive slaves. Brown urged the forty-four black members to resist, by violence if necessary, the clutches of the slave-catchers. While in Springfield, he met Frederick Douglass, and he outlined his "plan" for a future slave insurrection.[49]

Brown's initial national notice came in 1856 in strife-ridden Kansas. In retaliation for the "sack of Lawrence," he supervised the hacking to death of five pro-slavery men. In Springfield the next year, he spoke before a small but enthusiastic audience at Hampden Hall. He was looking for emigrants to Kansas, the right kind of men, "brave, temperate, strong, educated, and moral" men, who were willing to place themselves under his command in an emergency.[50] In late spring of 1859, he stopped by the *Republican* office for a chat. Bowles noted his "hale and hearty appearance" and his long, patriarchal beard, and he described Brown to his readers as "the ubiquitous, incorrigible, implacable foe of slaveholders."[51]

In October of 1859, Brown made his most memorable appearance on the national scene. Its impact made his Kansas actions pale by comparison. With his sons and a small band of black and white supporters, Brown attacked Harpers Ferry, Virginia. Brown and his men successfully seized the federal arsenal housed in that scenic town. Brown hoped that a general slave uprising would result or that a sectional crisis would develop in which slavery would ultimately be destroyed. Blood was shed, and two of his sons died in the raid. The slave uprising never materialized. Thirty-six hours after the revolt began, it ended. A company of United States marines had arrived in the evening and stormed the engine house in which Brown and his four remaining raiders were stockaded. Brown was struck by the light dress sword of the leader of the commando raid, and luckily the thrust hit either belt buckle or bone. Brown then was knocked unconscious by another marine. Colonel Robert E. Lee had a doctor look after him for his minor wounds, and then he was taken into custody in the armory paymaster's office. After a brief trial, Brown was found guilty and he died on the gallows.[52]

Bowles thought the raid was America's greatest civil insurrection. He also believed it a "foolhardy expedition," and he was amazed that it inspired so much terror throughout the south.[53] He reported that southerners feared going to sleep at night, mortified by the prospect of being slain in bed by their "faithful servants."[54] Bowles assured his readers that the prospect of Brown being put to death was slim.[55] Bowles praised Brown effusively, calling him a hero, the symbol of truth, courage, and liberty.[56] He averred that history would prove Brown innocent of any crime.[57]

Springfield took Brown's death hard. He had made many friends during his residence in town and his subsequent visits. A memorial service was held at the "colored" Sanford Street church. A letter written from Brown to a Springfield woman was read and brought tears even to those "unaccustomed to weeping."[58] The next month, the *Republican* had a final comment on the Brown affair. Under a headline that read "THE MOST APPROPRIATE TOYS FOR SOUTHERN CHILDREN," Bowles commented on "Little wooden John Browns hanging upon the gallows, with cranks attached, by which the legs and arms may be made to jerk and dangle in a beautifully suggestive manner."[59]

The new session of Congress that followed Brown's insurrection was stormy. Sectional tensions were at a fever pitch. Mutual distrust was the order of the day. Southern leaders repeatedly declared that the south would not submit to Republican Party rule, as paranoia reigned in the land of cotton. Southerners saw abolitionists under every bed, behind every door. Pity the poor soul who uttered even a mildly disapproving word against the region or the "peculiar institution!"[60] Such was the atmosphere in much of the south on the eve of the 1860 presidential election.

The consensus in the north was that southerners were bluffing, that the steamy rhetoric was merely intended for home consumption, to strengthen southern politicians' standing among their own constituency. In early spring of 1860, Bowles scoffed at the notion of disunion: "There is nothing more ridiculous than the fears of disunion . . . as a consequence of a Republican triumph in the next presidential election."[61] In May, Bowles left Springfield to attend the Republican Party convention in Chicago. The convention was chaired by his friend and neighbor, George Ashmun. In transit, he wrote that, although there may be a fight over the nominee—Bowles supported Governor Nathaniel Banks of Massachusetts[62]—the party was united on policy.[63]

Springfield Republican readers closely followed the convention proceedings. First, they were told the nominee would be Bates, McLean, Wade, Lincoln, or Banks, but not Cameron.[64] The next day, they learned that Lincoln was gaining favor.[65] The day after, Bowles' readers were informed that William Seward was gaining strength and was probably the nominee that day.[66] But on the 19th, they learned that it was not Seward after all, but Abraham Lincoln of Illinois, with Hannibal Hamlin of Maine his running mate. That evening, Bowles reported that "Chicago was in a blaze of glory . . . and the people are crazy with joy."[67]

Lincoln had impressed Bowles some twelve years earlier when he had heard him speak in Boston.[68] He was now even more enthusiastic: "Lincoln is a man of the most incorruptible integrity—firm as a rock against duplicity, dishonesty, and all dishonorable conduct, public and private."[69] Lincoln's election was assured when the Democratic Party, torn asunder over the slave issue, nominated two men: Stephen A. Douglas from its northern faction and John C. Breckenridge from its southern wing. True to its word, South Carolina bolted from the Union after Lincoln's election. Bowles' initial position was to let her go.[70] But as the situation at Fort Sumter deteriorated,[71] Bowles changed his stance, declaring that the federal government "cannot admit for a moment the destructive dogma that the Union can be broken up by one or more states. It cannot recognize South Carolina . . . as out of the Union."[72]

On April 12, at 4:30 a.m., as crowds applauded and wildly waved handkerchiefs, Fort Sumter was fired upon. The Civil War had begun.[73]

NOTES

1. Elting Morison, "The Election of 1860," *History of American Presidential Elections*, edited by Arthur M. Schlesinger, Jr., volume II, (New York Chelsea House), pp. 865-897.

2. Merriam, I:53.

3. *S.R.*, June 3, 1848.

4. The announcement of Bowles' appointment appeared in *S.R.*, August 25, 1848, p. 2, col. I.

5. Holman Hamilton, *Prologue to Conflict: The Crisis and Compromise of 1850* (New York: W. W. Norton, 1964).

6. Whitman Bennet, *Whittier, Bard of Freedom* (Chapel Hill: University of North Carolina Press, 1941), pp. 218-219.

7. *S.R.*, Extra, March 13, 1850. When Webster died on October 25, 1852, the entire *Springfield Republican* was printed with black borders. The practice was repeated in the following issue.

8. Ralph Corngold, *Two Friends of Man* (Boston: Little, Brown, 1950), p. 164.

9. Leonard Richards, *Gentlemen of Property and Standing: Anti-Abolitionist Mobs in America* (New York: Oxford University Press, 1970), pp. 63-64.

10. John Thomas, *The Liberator* (Boston: Little, Brown, 1963), p. 201.

11. Theresa Harrison, "George Thompson and the 1851 'Anti-Abolition' Riot," *Historical Journal of Western Massachusetts* (Spring 1976), p. 38.

12. *S.R.*, February 17, 1851, p. 2, col. II and col. V.

13. Ibid., January 10, 1851, p. 2, col. I.

14. Harrison, p. 40.

15. Ibid., pp. 41-43 and *S.R.*, February 19, 1851, p. 2, col. III.

16. Merriam, I:85.

17. *S.R.*, September 9, 1851, p. 2, col. I.

18. Merriam, I:59.

19. *S.R.*, April 23, 1852, p. 2, col. I.

20. Merriam, I:60.

21. Thomas O'Connor, *The Disunited States: The Era of Civil War and Reconstruction*, second edition (New York: Harper and Row, 1978), pp. 53-54.

22. *S.R.*, February 8, 1854 and Robert Johannsen, *Stephen A. Douglas* (New York: Oxford University Press, 1973), pp. 401-464, passim.

23. Merriam, I:120 and Jane and William Pease, *The Fugitive Slave Law and Anthony Burns: A Problem in Law Enforcement* (New York: Crowell, 1975).

24. *S.R.*, June 3, 1854.

25. Merriam, I:133.

26. John Mulkern, "Western Massachusetts in the Know-Nothing Years: An Analysis of Voting Patterns," *Historical Journal of Western Massachusetts* (January 1980), p. 14.

27. *S.R.*, March 31, 1854.

28. Gardner to Bowles, September 17, 1855, Boston, Monday Morning, and undated, Dorchester, "Tuesday Morning, Early," Samuel Bowles Papers, Sterling Memorial Library, Yale University.

29. *S.R.*, November 15, 1854. See also Dale Baum, *The Civil War Party System: The Case of Massachusetts, 1848-1876* (Chapel Hill: University of North Carolina Press, 1984), chapter 2.

30. *S.R.*, June 16, 1855, p. 4, col. I, and Jeter Allen Isely, *Horace Greeley and the Republican Party* (Princeton: Princeton University Press, 1947), pp. 52-53. Bowles signed his column "Quien Sabe."

31. Merriam, I:139.

32. James MacGregor Burns, *The Vineyard of Liberty* (New York: Vintage, 1983), p. 553.

33. Merriam, I:139.

34. *S.R.*, July 7, 1855.

35. Richard Lucid, editor, *The Journal of Richard Henry Dana Jr.*, volume II (Cambridge: Belknap Press of Harvard University Press, 1968), p. 677.

36. Merriam, I:143.

37. Ibid., p. 144.

38. William R. Brock, *Conflict and Transformation: The United States, 1844-1877* (New York: Penguin Books, 1973), p. 149 and David Donald, *Charles Sumner and the Coming of the Civil War* (New York: Knopf, 1960), pp. 278-311, passim.

39. *S.R.*, May 24, 1856.

40. Merriam, I:149; *S.R.*, February 27, 1856, p. 2, col. III; and Hooker, pp. 82-83.

41. *S.R.*, June 10, 1856.

42. Ibid., June 9, 1856.

43. Allen Nevins, *Fremont, Pathmaker of the West* (New York: D. Appleton-Century, 1939).

44. Merriam, I:151.

45. *S.R.*, November 1, 1856.

46. Don E. Fehrenbacher, *The Dred Scott Case* (New York: Oxford University Press, 1978). Emerson's widow later married C. C. Chaffee, a Springfield congressman.

47. Merriam, I:222.

48. *S.R.*, March 16, 1857.

49. Stephen B. Oates, *To Purge This Land With Blood: A Biography of John Brown* (New York: Harper and Row, 1970), pp. 51-69. Brown lived in three spots during his residence in Springfield: The Massasoit House, Ferry Street (then called Cyprus Street), and Franklin Street. See Frances Gagnon, "John Brown, Abolitionist," *Springfield Journal*, March 7, 1985, pp. 1 and 5.

50. *S.R.*, February 20, 1857, p. 2, col. IV.

51. Ibid., June 3, 1859, p. 2, col. I.

52. Oates, pp. 290-352, passim. One key Brown supporter was Franklin Sanborn, later a *Springfield Republican* editor. His role is explained in Jeffrey Rossbach, *Ambivalent Conspirators: John Brown, The Secret Six and A Theory of Slave Violence* (Philadelphia: The University of Pennsylvania Press, 1984).

53. *S.R.*, October 19, 1859, p. 2, col. I.

54. Ibid., October 20, 1859, p. 2, col. I.

55. Ibid., November 2, 1859, p. 2, col. I. After Brown was captured, he sought legal help from Springfield attorney Rueben Chapman. He asked Chapman if he would be his counsel or to recommend someone else. He was willing to pay Chapman $250 and other "personal property." Chapman was busy on court business and did not go to Virginia. See John Brown to Rueben Chapman, October 21, 1859, in Green, p. 514.

56. *S.R.*, December 2, 1859, p. 2, col. I.

57. Ibid., December 3, 1859, p. 4, col. I.

58. Ibid., December 3, 1859, p. 8, col. I.

59. Ibid., January 19, 1860, p. 2, col. V.

60. Allen Nevins, *The Emergence of Lincoln: Prologue to Civil War 1859-1861*, volume II (New York: Scribners, 1950), p. 107.

61. *S.R.*, April 11, 1860, p. 2, col. I.

62. Ibid., May 9, 1860, p. 2, col. I.

63. Ibid., May 14, 1860, p. 2, col. II.

64. Ibid., May 16, 1860, p. 2, col. III.

65. Ibid., May 17, 1860, p. 2, col. II.

66, Ibid., May 18, 1860, p. 2, col. II.

67. Ibid., May 19, 1860, p. 4. col. IV and Bowles to Wife, May 18, 1860 in Merriam, I:303. After Lincoln was nominated, he wrote to George Ashmun to clear up the matter of how he spelled his name. It was "Abraham" and not "Abram" he assured Ashmun. See Green, p. 518.

68. *S.R.*, September 14, 1848.

69. Ibid., May 23, 1860, p. 2, col. II.

70. Ibid., November 15, 1860, p. 2, col. I and Merriam, I:275.

71. Richard Current, *Lincoln and The First Shot* (Philadelphia: Lippincott, 1963).

72. *S.R.*, January 5, 1861.

73.   Roy Nichols, *The Stakes of Power* (New York: Hill and Wang, 1961), p. 99.

CHAPTER III

A PERFECTIONIST AT WORK

As the guns blazed in the Civil War, Bowles looked back with satisfaction at the progress of his *Republican*. Circulation gains were impressive; the combined totals for the daily and weekly grew to over eighteen thousand, and two thousand subscribers lived outside New England. His readers lived in every state except Mississippi, and in every territory but Utah. The daily *Republican* had a greater pro rata circulation than any other newspaper in the town or city of its publication.[1] The *Republican's* circulation gains occurred as the paper improved and enlarged its appearance. In late 1848, a column was added to each page, which was lengthened by two inches.[2] Several years later, the paper added another column, making seven altogether.[3] In early 1855, a new, clearer type appeared and the paper was enlarged once again.[4] There was more news, and advertisements, than ever before.

Bowles was a combative editor. Thin-skinned, he did not take lightly criticism of himself or his newspaper. He was fond of saying that "the *Republican* was one thing and Sam Bowles was another."[5] But no one believed it. Sam Bowles and the *Springfield Republican* were inextricably entwined. No other newspaper of the time embodied more of its editor's heart and soul than the *Springfield Republican*.

Bowles was a perfectionist. He rarely admitted error. He once commented to a colleague that he sympathized with a Boston editor to whom a man complained, " 'Your paper says that I hanged myself, and I want you to take it back.' 'No,' said the editor. 'We're not in the habit of doing that, but we will say that the rope broke and you escaped.' "[6]

Bowles was particularly feisty with rival editors. One headline read "THE POST— Its Forgeries and Perversions." Bowles declared

33

that "Here was a direct, inexcusable, plainly stated falsehood."[7] Later, he contended that the *Post's* editor "did not half read the article he criticized, did not understand any of it, and was disposed to misrepresent what he thought he understood."[8]

Bowles always liked to get in the last word. The editor of the *Northampton Courier* reprinted an item from the *Republican*. "The *Springfield Republican* says that tables for seventy-five were set for the Sumner supper . . . and that only half that number of persons were present, making the number in attendance thirty-seven and a half!" Bowles countered that the *Republican* account was correct. There were thirty-seven men and the editor of the *Courier*.[9] When criticized for inconsistencies, he snapped that it did not bother him that the paper sometimes contradicted itself. His business was reporting the news of the day and doing the same the next day. That was one of the paper's "fascinations."[10]

No other editor worked as hard as Bowles. Even when away from his office, he still had his mind on the paper. He ate, drank, and slept it. A friend recalled, "Zeal for his business, zeal, burning zeal for his newspaper which was verily to him bone of his bone, and flesh of his flesh, ate him up."[11] He once apologized to his friend, Henry Dawes, for not writing sooner, but he knew that Dawes would understand, as he had been at work for forty-two continuous hours.[12] Another friend, Edward Gillet of Westfield, scolded Bowles about his overwork. Bowles thanked him for his concern, but told him that he was not about to change his work habits. "When my friends point out that I am working toward a breakdown, they seem to think that is to influence my action. Not at all! I have got the lines drawn, the current flowing and by throwing my weight here now, I can count for something. If I make a long break or parenthesis to get strong, I shall lose my chance. No man is living a life that is worth living unless he is willing, if need be, to die for somebody or something—at least to die a little."[13] Gordon M. Fisk, editor of the *Palmer Journal*, met with Bowles one afternoon at the *Republican* building. Shortly afterward, he met William S. Robinson, the Boston correspondent for the *Republican*, who signed his columns "Warrington." "I've just left Sam Bowles upstairs," said Fisk, "wearing his life out looking for a turned letter in the *Republican*."[14]

Bowles did not tolerate laziness, or even a moderate pace. He expected his subordinates to work almost as hard as he did. One prospective reporter's parents were warned by James T. Robinson, editor of the *North Adams Transcript*, not to let their son work for Bowles for fear he would "kill him" with hard work.[15] Bowles was indeed a hard taskmaster. His poor health often left him moody, and his employees often bore the brunt of his misery.[16] He inspired respect—and not a little fear. He could be fatherly and brutal to his young reporters all in the same day. Once, Bowles asked a cub reporter to condense some copy. Working frightfully, he gave the shortened version back to the chief. Bowles took one look at it, cried "Bah!" and proceeded to mark it over furiously. "Read it now," he exclaimed. "Have I omitted anything essential?" The chastened tyro agreed; only the excess verbiage was gone.[17] Bowles' one fault, a staffer recalled, was his inability to commend work well-done.[18]

Bowles detested excess verbiage and pretentious prose. He demanded from his reporters writing that was clear, direct, and easily understandable.[19] He chided the *New York Times*, which prided itself on its "fine writing." He reprinted a "specimen of the perfection" which its financial column had achieved: "It will check to some degree the phlebomotic drainage of the yellow current that vivifies the veins of our commerce and to that extent delay or modify any morbific crisis likely to be induced by the febrile system of stimulation now predominant."[20]

In an editorial entitled "What Shall We Print?" Bowles took issue with critics who felt that only good or positive news should be published in the *Republican*. Bowles argued that young men and women must also be made aware of the harsh realities of life. Sin and vice, disgusting and disagreeable things, must be covered. An editor, he believed, must never be polite and nice at the cost of the truth.[21] Bowles felt strongly that his readers deserved nothing less than all the facts, even at the cost of endangering friendships and family ties. In 1856, an illegal prize fight took place in Springfield while he was out of town covering a political convention. Springfield's gentlemen of property and standing were among the spectators, including several relatives of Mrs. Bowles. He returned home shortly before the trial commenced. One night as the couple sat on the front doorstep, his wife asked, "Can't you let this thing drop? If you publish these young men's names, it will wound and alienate a great many of our friends." Bowles looked directly into his wife's eyes and responded,

"Mary, I have considered it all, most thoughtfully and conscientiously. The blame must be given where it is deserved. This is the time to put an end to prize-fighting in Springfield."[22] The trial received complete coverage in the *Republican*. Attendants at the prize fight were called as witnesses and names were named. Family relations were severely strained and not soon healed.[23]

Bowles wrote often about the newspaper business. He enjoyed sharing with his readers his philosophy of editing and his thoughts about the newspaper business. He took umbrage at those who demeaned the role of a newspaper editor, and he scoffed at those who thought a newspaper a mere compilation and a good pair of scissors the only necessity. Under an editor's skillful ministration, Bowles wrote, "the dry bones of isolated materials are not simply wired together, like the 'anatomy' in the office of the village doctor; they are clothed with beauty—they are throbbing with vitality . . . ."[24] Editing a newspaper, he pointed out to skeptics, was no easy task. He must "detect the truth from falsehood among rumors and speculations, to perceive what is probable and what otherwise." Most importantly, he must know "what to put in and what to leave out." Editing a newspaper, he stated positively, was much harder than writing for one. There are a lot of fine writers in the nation, but few good editors.[25]

Bowles aimed to make his paper lively and current.[26] Perish the thought that anyone consider it boring or dull! He was rarely happier than when told his paper was fresh weeks after publication date.[27] He was in the business of selling newspapers. The more he sold, the greater number of advertisers he attracted. Bowles was never indifferent to making money, lots of it.

No one man, however, not even Samuel Bowles, could run a newspaper alone. Bowles was fortunate in having an able staff by his side over the course of his long career. In late 1854, Clark W. Bryan was added to the *Republican* staff. Previously, Bryan had edited the *Berkshire Courier*, based in Great Barrington, Massachusetts, a small town some sixty miles west of Springfield. Bryan had worked for Bowles gathering election returns in southern Berkshire County. He was bright, loyal, of placid nature, and, like his boss, addicted to his work. Bryan typically worked in the office from 11 a.m. to 4 p.m. At four, he left the office, not to go home, but rather to the railroad station to pick up the Boston newspapers. He then returned to the

Republican building and worked until two in the morning. Unsurprisingly, after about a year of this schedule, he suffered a severe breakdown. The two men enjoyed each other's company and often took morning horseback rides together.[28]

In 1846, Joseph E. Hood, a quiet, unassuming man, became assistant editor. An Amesbury, Massachusetts native, the erudite Hood was a friend of the poet John Greenleaf Whittier. A Dartmouth College graduate, Hood turned to journalism after originally intending a career in the ministry. His overwork contributed to his chronic poor health. He and Bowles were attuned philosophically and ideologically. A colleague commented that "Bowles would talk to Hood for five minutes, giving him points for an article, and then go off, and Hood would work it out perfectly."[29]

Both Bryan and Hood were of inestimable value to Bowles. But one man, Josiah G. Holland, was indispensable. Holland joined the *Republican* in 1849. Several years later, he bought an interest in the paper for $3,500. Holland was a prolific writer who achieved initial fame for his "Titcomb Letters," a series that discussed such themes as "the mutual duties of husbands and wives, of laborers and employers, and the proper conduct of young men and women."[30] Holland also wrote a detailed *History of Western Massachusetts*, and a very popular biography of Abraham Lincoln.[31] He was sentimental and high-strung, but he was also a bit of a prig. He often wrote sympathetically about the common people, but he refused to personally have anything to do with them, finding fault with their moral standards.[32] Unlike Holland, Bowles would talk to anybody. Holland once wrote Bowles on their relationship: "We're not enough alike to ever be intimate friends. I mean friends who wholly unbosom themselves to each other. There has always been an unseen bar between us that keeps us apart. It grows out of our diverse natures I think . . . ." He added, however, that, nevertheless, Bowles was as good a friend as a man could have.[33] The two always addressed each other, in both public and private, as "Mr. Bowles" and "Dr. Holland."[34]

Bowles' success in Springfield did not go unnoticed. In December 1856, he was asked if he was interested in starting a new newspaper in Philadelphia. Bowles was flattered and wrote his close friend Charles Allen of Greenfield that he felt "as did the bashful boy, whose father was urging him to go and marry a certain girl of the neighborhood. 'I was married—your mother was married—and you must expect to be.' 'But,' blubbered the youth, 'you married mother, but you want me to go and marry a strange gal.'" He concluded that he was certain he could edit a newspaper in Massachusetts, but that he had some doubts about that "strange gal in Philadelphia."[35] Bowles wrote Allen again several days later, after meeting with a representative from Philadelphia. He expressed doubts that the plan would actually materialize, and he was right.[36]

A few months later, however, the *Republican* announced a startling development: Samuel Bowles had accepted editorial charge of the *Boston Traveller*. It added that while Bowles would no longer have any control over the *Republican's* contents, he would retain his "proprietary interest in the establishment . . . ." Dr. Holland was left in charge, with Hood and Bryan as his right-hand men. The *Traveller* owners gave Bowles fourteen thousand dollars in capital stock and a salary of three thousand dollars per year.[38] Bowles obviously saw a great opportunity. He had often complained about the difficulties in editing a superior newspaper in a "provincial town." This was his chance, he must have thought; perhaps the one of a lifetime. Yet, he obviously had his doubts; why else would he retain his ownership of the *Republican* and, more importantly, leave his wife and children in Springfield?[39]

The *Boston Atlas* and the *Telegraph and Chronicle* had just been consolidated in the *Boston Traveller*, thus giving Bowles a large staff of fifteen, mostly experienced correspondents.[40] Bowles was determined to make the *Traveller* one of the nation's leading newspapers.[41] Yet after barely a month at the helm, Bowles expressed some misgivings. He wrote Mary that he often thought himself a fool for leaving "old Springfield." He was thankful, he added, that he could *afford to fail*, but resolved that he did not intend to.[42] Bowles demanded loyalty from his new editors, and support from the owners. The owners, however, quarreled over the shape and direction of the new paper. Money that Bowles understood would be put into the new operation was not forthcoming. Moreover, his independence was being undermined by the owners' allegiance to Governor Gardner. Bowles was also upset by the lack of a cohesive internal organization.[43]

That summer, Bowles spent much of his time seeking to extricate himself from the *Traveller*. Fortunately, one of his best friends, Charles Allen of Greenfield, was also an able lawyer who was more than happy to aid his friend. Bowles wrote Allen that he could afford to lose what he invested in the *Traveller*, but did not want to endanger anything he had in Springfield.[44] By mid-September of 1857, Bowles managed to sever his ties with the *Traveller*. With a loud sigh of relief, he returned to his home town. After a brief vacation with Allen and his sister, Bowles resumed control of the *Republican*. Holland voluntarily relinquished his editorial charge to Bowles, sold his small interest in the paper, and withdrew from all editorial duties except writing.[45] Physical health in part restored, with an ego slightly tattered, Bowles threw himself back into the day-to-day operations of his *Republican*. He had learned his lesson; future offers to leave Springfield were never again seriously entertained.

Bowles' health, barely adequate under favorable conditions, suffered greatly under the stresses of his stint in Boston. He was, as he put it, "terribly used up."[46] He realized he needed periods of rest on a regular basis, a chance to get away—but not too far away—where he could relax. He found his haven some twenty-five miles north-northeast, in Amherst. Bowles was no stranger to the town that he wrote, "furnishes the beauty—the world comes to adore." Since 1849, he had been reporting on Amherst College commencements. In 1858, he came to Amherst on a fairly regular basis.[47]

He relished the company of the town's most prominent family, the Dickinsons. Edward Dickinson, prominent lawyer, former Congressman, and family patriarch, was always grateful to the *Republican* for its unswerving support. His son Austin and daughter-in-law Susan Gilbert Dickinson, were Bowles' closest friends in town. Susan later recalled to her children that Bowles was known to them as "Uncle Sam." It was difficult, she explained, to put in words how much his friendship had meant to them. "He was a true knight, with the fine flower of courtesy on his invisible shield." The threesome would spend hours engrossed and delighting in each other's company, often until "long after midnight." She was clearly captivated by his presence. When they spoke, she later recalled, "Even if the matter discussed was dry, as his favorite scheme for abridging all legal forms and usages in our courts . . . he made this subject stirring and fascinating. His range of topics was unlimited."[48]

Bowles and the Dickinsons regularly visited and corresponded. They expressed mutual concern about each other's state of health, and they exchanged Christmas presents. They were totally at ease in each other's company and, on occasion, teased and were playfully sarcastic. After a brief illness, Susan knew he was feeling better, she told him, because he was "getting back into [his] god-like attitude again."[49] Bowles would have visited the couple more but for his staggering work-load and, perhaps more importantly, his wife's being ill at ease with the Dickinsons.[50]

Mary Bowles never fit in among the Dickinson entourage. She was a simple woman, with simple tastes. Modest, and not the least bit intellectual, she was defensive in the rarified air of Amherst, and apt to blurt out the wrong things. One visit, for example, was a disaster. Shortly afterwards, Bowles wrote Austin asking for his understanding: "you must make some allowances" for Mary's "peculiarities—and judge her by what she means, rather always than by what she says. Her very timidity and want of self-reliance gives her a sharper utterance . . . her Amherst visit—it did not turn out so pleasantly . . . . Of course, the fault was mainly hers, but it was also partly mine. I did not manage her as she wanted to be managed . . . . But do not judge Mary too harshly. She . . . needs help."[51] In subsequent visits, Bowles usually came alone. He wrote Austin that Mary would not come—and could hardly be expected to—"since Sue has not been to see her even though she has been to Springfield two or three times."[52] The sensitive Mary must have also been shaken by gossip that characterized her husband's relationship with Sue as "questionable."[53]

Austin and Susan Dickinson respected, admired, and were thoroughly charmed by Bowles. Emily Dickinson also loved him.[54] The reclusive poetic genius was powerfully attracted to the tall, slightly stooped, full-bearded editor with eyes, as she saw them, like "isolated comets."[55] One year, the Bowles' sent her a Christmas present, Theodore Parker's *The Two Christmas Celebrations.*[56] Samuel liked Emily, but he also thought, along with almost everyone else, that she was an eccentric. As a result, he never really took her seriously. Bowles would have been shocked had he known her true feelings toward him. When he suffered, she suffered. She was anguished when he was in pain. Her letters to him showed "a concern for his health that went far beyond the requirements even of close friendship."[57] Her letter of consolation to Mary Bowles in 1860, after her third still-born child in the past five years, was hardly reflective of casual acquaintanceship.[58] Dickinson the poet was rebuffed professionally by the man she loved. Only five of her poems

Samuel Bowles, courtesy of the Springfield City Library.

made it into the *Republican*. All were published anonymously, with altered titles and with editing either by Bowles or a member of his staff.[59] The proud poet was outraged by the unauthorized alterations.

Bowles never did like poetry very much. The type he tolerated was plain and simple, like the poem he subsequently wrote, the only one that ever came from his pen. A female compositor in the *Republican* office came into the chief's office one day and asked him to write his signature in her book. Instead of merely signing his autograph, he penned in the following:

> "Our Lucy's album! Come and write
> Young men and maidens all;
> Put dainty thoughts in phrases trite,
> And make the pot hooks small.
> Lovers may write their hopes and fears
> On leaves of blushing hue;
> Wise women, getting into years
> Will scribble on the blue;
> While for the girls - why bless the dears!
> They've left the green for you.
> Pass round the book and let it claim
> Free gifts from generous souls
> An album only asks a name
> Here take it,
> > > Samuel Bowles"[60]

In July 1860, an article Bowles wrote entitled "When Should We Write" appeared in the *Republican*. He denigrated the type of writing he called "the literature of misery." Who was responsible for it? ". . . chiefly women may be, full of thought and feeling and fancy, but poor, lonely, and unhappy . . . ." He pointed out that "suffering is so seldom healthful . . . it too often clouds, withers, distorts."[61] Emily must have been devastated. Not only was it a personal rebuke, but it was also printed in a newspaper that the Dickinsons read religiously. Despite his insensitivity toward her work and feelings, Emily continued to think the world of Samuel Bowles. After her father's funeral, she refused to see anyone other than Bowles.[62]

In April 1862, Bowles and his brother Benjamin left for Europe on the English Cunard steamship *China*. He left, the *Republican* reported, for six months of "quiet life and recreation away from the present unusual excitements of newspaper life in this country." The trip, it was hoped, would "restore his nervous system"[63] Emily wrote Mary Bowles that "When the Best is gone—I know that other things are not of consequence . . . ."[64] To Samuel, she expressed the hope that "those Foreign people are kind and true to you" and that he would be the same person when he returned that she had "grieved for."[65]

Bowles undoubtedly gave little thought to Emily Dickinson as he prepared for his European voyage. Weary and exhausted, Europe excited him although he had reservations about leaving the *Republican* for such a long period with the nation in its greatest time of crisis. He was relieved, however, when Dr. Holland agreed to take over the paper in his absence.[66] On the eve of his departure, watching a blinding snowstorm from the warmth of his room at the Brevoort House in New York, he wrote Mary that "parting with home and its nearer and dearer ones" was a "hard strain."[67] He was off on the longest journey of his life.

NOTES

1.   *S.R.*, June 18, 1860, p. 2, col. II.

2.   Ibid., September 1, 1848, p. 2, col. I.

3.   Ibid., July 1, 1851, p. 2, col. I.

4.   Ibid., February 3, 1855, p. 1, col. I.

5.   Henry M. Whitney, *New Englander and Yale Review*, February 1886, pp. 97-107.

6. Elizabeth Ryan, "Samuel Bowles: Pioneer in Independent Journalism," Mount Holyoke College Honors Paper, 1936, p. 6.

7. *S.R.*, September 25, 1851, p. 2, col. IV.

8. Ibid., January 8, 1852, p. 2, col. I. See also *S.R.*, July 27, 1853, p. 2, col. I for a scathing attack on the rival *Springfield Post* for stealing articles.

9. Ibid., May 8, 1851, p. 2, col. IV.

10. Hooker, p. 59.

11. Unsigned article, *London Spectator*, July 24, 1886, pp. 993-994.

12. Bowles to Henry L. Dawes, November 10, 1856 in Dawes Papers, Library of Congress. See also Bowles to William Claflin, June 10, 1870, Rutherford B. Hayes Presidential Center, Fremont, Ohio.

13. Merriam, I:67.

14. Solomon Bulkley Griffin, *People and Politics Observed by a Massachusetts Editor* (Boston: Little, Brown and Company, 1923), p. 92.

15. Ibid., p. 93.

16. Merriam, I:136.

17. William H. Rideing, *Many Celebrities and a Few Others* (Garden City, NY: Doubleday, Page and Company, 1912), p. 37.

18. Griffin, p. 27.

19. Despite his admonition about excess verbiage, he often ran stories of several thousand words.

20. *S.R.*, September 12, 1859, p. 2, col. II.

21. Ibid., February 4, 1857, p. 2, col. I.

22. Merriam, I:71; *S.R.*, May 25, 1859, p. 2, col. I.

23. Merriam, I:72.

24. *S.R.*, June 9, 1860, p. 4, col. II.

25. Merriam, I:172.

26. *S.R.*, December 23, 1851, p. 2, col. I.

27. Nathaniel Banks to Samuel Bowles, January 23, 1856 in Bowles Papers, Sterling Memorial Library, Yale University.

28. Merriam, I:102-104.

29. Ibid., pp. 105-109.

30. Hooker, p. 52.

31. Holland's *The Life of Abraham Lincoln* appeared in 1866 and sold more than 100,000 copies. See Stephen B. Oates, *Abraham Lincoln: The Man Behind the Myths* (New York: Harper and Row, 1984), p. 5.

32. Merriam, I:63. For a detailed biographical sketch of Holland, see *S.R.*, August 17, 1867, p. 3, col. III.

33. Holland to Bowles, April 2, 1860, Bowles Papers.

34. Merriam, I:64.

35. Bowles to Allen, December 21, 1856, in Merriam, I:177.

36. Bowles to Allen, December 25, 1856, in Merriam, I:177-178.

37. *S.R.*, April 4, 1857, p. 4, col. I.

38. Bowles to Dawes (no date given, but probably February or March, 1857), Dawes Papers.

39. Hooker, p. 85.

40. Bowles to Allen, April 19, 1857 in Merriam, I:212.

41. Ibid., I:181.

42. Bowles to Wife, April 26, 1857 in Merriam, I:212. One journalist recalled that Bowles' "grand scheme for establishing a great metropolitan journal in Boston" failed because Boston did not want a quality newspaper. See Charles T. Congdon, *Reminiscences of a Journalist* (Boston: James R. Osgood and Company, 1880), p. 210. The *Republican's* Boston correspondent, "Warrington," wrote that Bowles was resented because he came down from Springfield "like the wolf on the fold." See Mrs. William S. Robinson, *Warrington Pen Portraits: A Collection of Personal and Political Reminiscences From 1848-1876* (Boston: Lee and Shepard, 1877), p. 84. Manton Marble was the man Bowles replaced as editor-in-chief. Marble was demoted to literary editor. Bowles criticized Marble's book reviews as too elevated in moral tone. They argued and Bowles reduced space for literary notices. Marble resigned as he could not work without independence, and he later became editor of the *New York*

World. See George T. McJimsey, *Genteel Partisan: Manton Marble 1834-1917* (Ames: Iowa State University Press, 1971), p. 11.

43. Frederick Hudson, *History of Journalism* (New York: Harper Brothers, 1873), p. 582. In an unsigned review of Merriam's book in the *Nation*, the author claims that Bowles was a laughingstock at the *Traveller* because of his "bumptiousness."

44. Merriam, I:294.

45. Ibid., p. 187.

46. Ibid., p. 295.

47. Richard Sewall, *The Life of Emily Dickinson* (New York: Farrar, Straus, and Giroux, 1974), p. 468.

48. Martha Dickinson Bianchi, *Emily Dickinson, Face to Face* (Boston: Houghton Mifflin, 1932), p. 281. Bowles' range of topics was indeed almost unlimited, if not often rather shallow. Bowles read widely—it was his job— but never deeply.

49. Susan Dickinson to Bowles, December 25, 1861 in Jay Leyda, *The Years and Hours of Emily Dickinson* (New Haven: Yale University Press, 1960), vol. II, p. 41.

50. Sewall, p. 472.

51. Bowles to Austin Dickinson, May 15, 1861 in Leyda, vol. II, p. 28.

52. Bowles to Austin Dickinson, February 2, 1863, ibid., p. 75.

53. Sewall, pp. 470-471. Ironically, both Mary Bowles and Susan Gilbert Dickinson grew up in the small town of Geneva, N.Y. There is no evidence they knew one another there.

54. Wendy Martin, *An American Triptych: Anne Bradstreet, Emily Dickinson, Adrienne Rich* (Chapel Hill: University of North Carolina Press, 1984), p. 99.

55. Sewall, p. 509.

56. Mary Bowles to Emily Dickinson, December 25, 1859 in Leyda, vol. I, p. 376.

57. Sewall, p. 481.

58. Emily Dickinson to Mary Bowles, May 27, 1859 in Leyda, vol. I, p. 369.

59. Sewall, p. 475.

60. Scrapbooks, Springfield City Library, Local History Room, volume 25, p. 18.

61. Ruth Miller, *The Poetry of Emily Dickinson* (Middletown, Conn: Wesleyan University Press, 1968), pp. 163-164.

62. Polly Longsworth, *Emily Dickinson: Her Letter to the World* (New York: Thomas Crowell, 1965), p. 138. Bowles took charge of arrangements for Edward Dickinson's funeral.

63. *S.R.*, April 9, 1862.

64. Emily Dickinson to Mary Bowles, mid-May?, 1862 in Leyda, vol. II, p. 58.

65. Emily Dickinson to Samuel Bowles, mid-June?, 1862 in Leyda, vol. II, p. 61.

66. Merriam, I:315.

67. Ibid., p. 340.

CHAPTER IV

TRAVELS EAST AND WEST

On April 23, the ailing editor arrived in Liverpool, after a rough voyage. He agreed with Dr. Johnson that "a man was wiser to go to prison than to sea. The independence and comfort were greater, besides avoiding the danger of drowning." Bowles promised his loyal readers an occasional "gossiping personal letter," but also reminded them that this was a "tour for health" so his writing would be limited lest the trip "cheat its purpose."[1]

England fascinated Bowles; he wrote that in some ways he already knew half the English people through the works of Thackeray, Dickens, and the magazine *Punch*. Bowles, a Unitarian, "sadly mixed up" his waiters and the ministers of the Church of England. "They dress just alike, but the waiters are more impressive of manner and brighter." One clergyman he heard at Westminster, Bowles thought, would do better "pouring beer in a country inn than in disgusting and befogging people from a pulpit."[2]

He wrote Mary that he was feeling better—at least better than when he left home. He was "thoroughly fatigued physically every day," but sleeping well at night. "England is beautiful," he wrote; "It is literally a garden. The hedges, the evergreens, the ivy, the flowers are rich with rural beauty." He concluded by telling Mary how much he missed her, that it was "a constant fret" not having her by his side. He was grateful, however, that she did not have to undergo the "torture and discomfort" of the voyage.[3]

Bowles enjoyed the company of his younger brother, Benjamin, who also wrote an occasional letter back to the *Republican*.[4] Benjamin loved his older brother and was somewhat in awe of him. He could not have been pleased, however, by one item Samuel chose to relate to his readers. One afternoon, it seems, the brothers were riding in Wales. Benjamin was sure a "stout, buxom lass threw him a kiss from the field where she was at work." But the elder brother saw it differently. "As she was shoveling manure from a wheel-barrow it seemed as if she was only spitting on her hands to take a firmer hold of her work."[5] Before he left Great Britain, Bowles visited Shakespeare's home. He was disappointed: "Don't it let down the romance of Stratford-on-Avon a trifle . . . to know that its chief modern distinction lies in the extent and excellence of its manufactories of ale?"[6]

After three weeks in England, Bowles left for France. As he travelled, he was determined to maintain a healthful routine, and to ease his "abused brain." He retired between ten and eleven and arose between seven and nine. He ate bread and butter (better than any in America), along with either eggs, fruit (three pounds of grapes on one morning), or a small portion of meat. He washed it down with weak coffee. Breakfast was followed by four or five hours of activities and sight-seeing and, sometimes, shopping. For lunch he ate more bread and butter with fruit. His usual dinner fare was soup, beef or mutton, more bread and butter, and some beer or wine. A long walk typically followed dinner.[7]

Paris fascinated Bowles. It was the "finishing off school of the Devil," yet also "the very vestibule of Heaven." "You pays your money and you has your choice," he told his readers, "and nowhere is the choice wider than here." As for the Parisian people, he thought them "gay rather than happy, volatile rather than sensual." He commended the city on its appearance; it was a clean city, certainly cleaner than New York or London.[8]

Next on Bowles' itinerary were the Netherlands and Germany. A short stay in Holland was enough for him to confidently characterize the Dutch as a "clean, virtuous, enterprising, sensible people." In his brief stay in Germany, he was told he had to see the cathedral with the eleven thousand virgins in Cologne. "They are an army who went out to do battle for the Lord centuries ago," Bowles wrote home, "and were slaughtered by his barbaric enemies, and now their bones and skulls line the walls of an old church, packed like cordwood or somtimes fantastically woven into crosses or pious words." Bowles was disgusted; he liked to believe in virgins, but thought eleven thousand were "too much . . . to put your faith in."[9]

His favorite European country, the one in which he spent the most time—some two months—was Switzerland. "Switzerland, if you come near to her, lasts, while the rest of Europe is lost in your soul or only remembered as a faint dream."[10] Bowles enjoyed the "starry heavens" and the "pure, fresh air that sets the soul free from the flesh,"[11] He was dazzled by the view from Gorner Grat, over ten thousand feet in elevation. He was enraptured by what he saw; the view was "the grandest, the greatest, the most sublime . . . ."[12] Lake Geneva was gorgeous, its water so "exquisitely pure and blue." He added that "no matter how much dirt is thrown into it, it turns all to purity and crystal."[13] Switzerland obviously agreed with him. His health there was improved and his nights, as he put it, were "not at all profaned by wakefulness." His only unpleasant memory took place in church, when he was forced to listen to a "stupid, unelevating sermon, all about the brazen serpent, the Israelites, and the severity of God!" Bowles was so "disappointed and disgusted," he resolved not to give a cent. His courage failed him, however, at the appearance of the plate-holder, and he "gave in, and paid."[14]

In November of 1862, Bowles returned to Springfield and to a country torn apart by civil war. The Civil War brought death and destruction, suffering and sacrifice. It also brought prosperity to Samuel Bowles, the *Republican*, and the city of Springfield. The war stimulated newspaper reading as had no other event in United States history. The public appetite for news from the battlefield was practically insatiable. Few people, north or south, were without at least one relative in the military. The *Daily Republican's* circulation increased one hundred per cent during the war.[15] "Extra" or evening editions of the paper were printed as events warranted.[16] Twice a week, the *Republican* expanded to eight pages, accommodating its increased advertising.[17]

The Armory's growth was phenomenal. Initially, the facility was unprepared for a protracted conflict, as production had even been curtailed in the 1850s. An obvious lack of materials and skilled personnel existed.[18] After Fort Sumter, plans were set in motion to hire more men and increase production. The work force increased by thousands beyond its two hundred man base. In 1861, the Armory produced eight hundred rifles. By 1864, its monthly production was an incredible twenty-six thousand.[19] Interested observers were amazed at the success of Springfield's most prominent institution.[20]

The city itself grew and prospered. By war's end, the population had increased by half, up to twenty-two thousand.[21] The city became overcrowded; housing shortages developed and rental prices doubled and in some cases tripled. Boarding houses charged an exorbitant fifteen dollars a week. Supply, however, gradually began to catch up with demand and by 1865 the housing crisis ended.[22]

Meanwhile, the partially reinvigorated editor prepared to re-enter the political maelstrom. Bowles had some initial doubts about Lincoln. At one point early on, he dubbed him a "simple Susan," and questioned his independence from the likes of Secretary of State William Seward and Treasury head Salmon Chase.[23] His early doubts, however, were soon dispelled as he praised Lincoln for being a "very shrewd and sensible man."[24] Bowles and the *Republican* regularly supported Lincoln's policies throughout the course of the conflict.[25] He agreed at the outset that the war was to save the Union first and foremost. But in 1863, he also declared it imperative "that slavery be destroyed."[26] Bowles was one of the first editors to recognize the Gettysburg Address for what it was, "a perfect gem, deep in feeling, compact in thought and expression"[27] In early 1865, he wrote that Congress' action in abolishing slavery through the Thirteenth Amendment to the Constitution was "a great day in our history."[28]

An even greater day for most Americans came a few months later. On April 9, Robert E. Lee surrendered the battered and scarred remnants of the Army of Northern Virginia at the Appomattox Court House. The war had taken 618,000 soldiers, including 360,000 Union troops and 258,000 Confederate.[29] Millions of others were physically and psychologically wounded. "The days of darkness and doubt are over; the days of gladness and victory have come," Bowles wrote. "There are vacant chairs and sad hearts everywhere," he added, "but the victory and the joy are for all. We honor the living heroes; we more than honor our fallen braves."[30]

The carnage left behind, Americans set about the difficult task of reconstruction. Samuel Bowles, however, had his mind on something else entirely. He was preparing for the second great trip of his life—some three thousand miles—this time not eastward, but westward across the continent. Bowles' travelling party consisted of Schuyler Colfax, Speaker of the House; William Bross, Lieutenant-Governor of Illinois; Albert D. Richardson, noted war correspondent of the *New York Tribune*; and George K. Otis, agent of Ben Holladay,

Schuyler Colfax, William Bross, and Samuel Bowles. Courtesy Springfield City
Library.

the creator of the Overland Stage Line. Otis was in charge of the group.[31] The long trek across the country took the men through Missouri, Kansas, Nebraska, Colorado, Utah, Nevada, California, Oregon, Washington, and back to San Francisco, where they returned home by ship via Panama. Colfax was also chairman of the House Committee on Post Offices and Post Roads, and he and Bowles were interested in western railroad growth, and especially the completion of a trans-continental line. The journey was like an "official junket," with Colfax and his crew "inspecting" the West.

Its most important accomplishment, however, was Samuel Bowles' *Across the Continent*, the most comprehensive account of the region of the time. The book contained thirty-two letters (first appearing in the *Springfield Republican* virtually verbatim) and eight "Supplementary Papers."[32] Bowles explained that the book was not "a Diary of a personal journey; nor a Guide book; nor a Hand-Book of statistics." He aimed to describe the scenery as vividly as possible and "portray the social and material developments of the several States and territories visited—their present and their future, their realization and their capacity." Bowles hoped to convince skeptical easterners that they would benefit from western development. The booster spirit infused much of his work; he was a major cheerleader of American nationalism.[33]

The eager men were prepared for all contingencies. They brought firearms to shoot game and ward off any unfriendly Indians. Sardines were stocked for those who couldn't digest bacon, and crackers for those "fastidious stomachs that rejected saleratus biscuit." An ample supply of "segars" were on hand for Colfax, and black tea was available for the "nervous newspaper men." There was even soap "for those so aristocratic as to insist on washing themselves on route."[34]

Bowles and his fellow-travellers got along quite well. For all the time spent together, much of it in a cramped coach, it was fortunate they did. Colfax, a short, slim widower from South Bend, Indiana, was a former printer and newspaper editor. His working habits were similar to that of Bowles. Bowles admired him greatly, and was shattered in later years when Colfax was implicated in political scandal. Bross was fifty-five, in excellent physical condition, and he had the most formal education of the group. Born in New Jersey, he liked to say that he could never be president as the Constitution requires the president to be a native of the nation. Richardson was a war hero, who had escaped from the Confederates after twenty months imprisonment. He enjoyed French brandy, carried excess baggage, couldn't play poker, and was a ladies' man. Otis was warm and out-going; his long experience and confident manner eased whatever anxieties the others had. As such, they forgave him his atrocious puns.[35]

Bowles knew what his readers wanted and he didn't disappoint them. Americans were fascinated by the "exotic" groups in their midsts, from the Indians to the Mormons to the newly-arriving Chinese. Bowles had plenty to say about each group, and in his usual way, held nothing back. He firmly believed in "Manifest Destiny" — the Godly-inspired duty to spread White Anglo-Saxon Protestant culture, with its blessings of liberty and democracy, across the land.[36] Bowles was furious that one group impeded the progress of the white race — the Indian.

Bowles admitted that Whites had plundered and cheated the Indians.[37] He also agreed that many of their problems stemmed from "the lust of coarse white men for their women" along with the nefarious dissemination of whiskey among them. He was certain that "mean and sordid whites" unnecessarily stirred the Indian's blood, leading to mischief and mayhem.[38] Nevertheless, Bowles insisted that the Indian was "false and barbaric, cunning and cowardly." He was "horrible in cruelty, the terror of women and children,[and] impenetrable to nearly every motive but fear . . . ."[39] Bowles argued that action had to be taken and quickly, for settlers and travellers could not be expected to continue to put up with "unexpected assaults and robbery."[40] Bowles offered an answer, a final solution — extermination. He preferred other methods of solving the problem, but reluctantly concluded that if they did not act quickly to behave peacefully, then they had to die.[41]

Bowles' attitude towards the Mormons was quite different. After his first day in Salt Lake City, Bowles understood why the Mormons saw themselves as a chosen people. He was astounded by the agricultural productivity and the beauty of the area. He praised their "industry, ingenuity, and endurance." That they made the desert bloom was a testimony to their superior abilities and dedication.[42] Bowles and his party met Mormon leader Brigham Young, a young-looking and vigorous man of sixty-four, with "a mouth and chin betraying a great and determined will." He was a handsome man, perhaps, but lacking charisma. He was "cool and quiet" in demeanor, had "strong and original ideas," but, to Bowles' surprise, he used "bad grammar."[43] He was less impressed with the rest of the Mormon hierarchy. They looked like, Bowles wrote, they had "gone to the same church and sat in the same pew without cushions; [and] borrowed the same weekly newspaper for forty years."[44]

Bowles was impressed with the Great Salt Lake, "a miniature ocean." It was so salty, he wrote, you can't sink; the body floats "as a cork on the surface." The East, he conceded, had nice "watering-places"—Newport, Saratoga, Sharon—but none of them were half as good as Salt Lake. So, he intoned, "ye votaries of fashion, ye rheumatic cripples, ye victims of scrofula and ennui, prepare to pack your trunk," and head on out to the Great Salt Lake.[45]

The somewhat puritanical editor was horrified by polygamy. Less than a quarter of all Mormons practiced it, he learned, but that was bad enough. "It . . . means the degradation of women. By it and under it, she becomes simply the servant and serf."[46] Polygamy "brutalizes man, teaching him to despise and domineer over his wives, over all women."[47] Bowles warned that living with polygamy, Mormon children could not help being debased. Fortunately, he discovered, the Mormon girls grew up indisposed to polygamy, "and seek husbands among the Gentiles rather than among their own faith."[48]

On Independence Day, 1865, after several months of often arduous travel, the men reached California. "Fifteen hundred miles of railroad, two thousand of staging, again sixty miles of railway, and then one hundred and fifty miles by steamboat down the Sacramento River, and the goal is reached, the Continent is spanned."[49]

Bowles noted the presence of large numbers of Chinese—some sixty to seventy thousand, he guessed—in California, and especially San Francisco. Their treatment shocked him; a Chinaman staking a claim was often told to "move on." If he resisted, he was killed. They were gunned down like sportsmen shooting their game in the woods. Their testimony in court was inadmissible against the white man.[50] The Chinese, Bowles noted, did not intend to stay in America. They came to work and, Bowles observed, they worked hard to make money and return home. The men came alone; the few women, according to Bowles, were prostitutes, whose customers were not just

Chinese, but also "base white men who patronize their wares as well . . . ." The Chinese did all the laundry for everyone, and "as they iron they squirt a fine spray of water from their mouths. They are fine house servants," he concluded, better than the Irish girls back East.[51]

Bowles was hardly impressed with their religion. He thought it "cheap, showy and idolatrous." They are a stoic people, he observed, without "the passion, good or bad, that marks the western races. Their two great vices are Opium smoking and gambling. They gamble everywhere; in house and shops, often to the accompaniment of their barbaric music."[52]

Bowles and his travelling companions accepted a dinner invitation from the "SIX CHINESE COMPANIES IN CALIFORNIA."[53] It must have been the most memorable eating experience of his life. The meal consisted of three different courses or "dinners," with a half-hour break between dinners. Chopsticks were used, but those who had trouble handling them were given a "yankee" fork. Each course contained twelve to twenty dishes, usually served one at a time. The main dishes for the first course were fried shark's fins, grated ham, stewed pigeon with bamboo soup, fish sinews with ham, stewed chicken with water cress, seaweed, stewed ducks and bamboo soup, spongecake, omelet cake, flower cake, banana fritters, bird nest soup, and tea. Bowles liked the tea.

Unbeknownst to the slightly nauseous editor, help was on the way. San Francisco's chief of police appeared, touched Bowles' shoulder, and informed him he had to leave and to bring his hat and coat. Bowles was puzzled. What had he done, he wondered, to break the law? Nothing. At the front door, a leading banker who had left the dinner earlier, met the mystified editor. "Bowles, I knew you were suffering, and were hungry—let us go and get something to eat—a good square meal!" Relieved and delighted, Bowles and his new friend went to a nearby American restaurant and ate some all-American food—meat and potatoes.[54]

Among the longest letters he wrote was "The Great Theme: The Pacific Railroad." An underlying purpose of the trip, he explained, was expediting the linkage of the transcontinental railroad. Everywhere he travelled, the same question was repeated, " 'When is the Railroad going to be completed?' Tender-eyed women, hard-fisted men—pioneers or missionaries, the martyrs and the successful," all wanted to know. Bowles urged the Congressmen to dedicate themselves to the task at hand. America had to be united to achieve its greatness. North and South now were, and it was time "to marry the Nation of the Atlantic [with] an equal, if not greater Nation of the Pacific."[55]

Bowles spent a lot of time in the mines and in new mining communities of the West. Austin, Nevada, only two years old when visited by Bowles, already had eight thousand inhabitants. Bowles was flabbergasted that the boom town had a French restaurant—and that it was so good. One evening, he and his comrades entered the Mammoth Saloon, where "Votaries of Bacchus, Gambrinus, Venus, or Cupid can spend an evening agreeably . . . ." Bowles was unimpressed; the sole representative of all these "proclaimed gods and goddesses," he wrote, "was a fat, coarse Jew girl . . . ."[56]

Bowles offered advice on mine investments. He warned his readers that every steamer brought speculators and adventurers back East "with mines to sell—good, bad, and indifferent—but mostly uncertain."[57] He illustrated his point by citing Fremont's problems in the mining business. "Why," said General Fremont, "when I came to California, I was worth nothing, and now I owe two millions of dollars!"[58] Bowles also detailed the intricate nature of mining. He described the physical processes of mining and economic factors such as cost-price ratios. He half-seriously warned his readers not to complain about the excessive dry facts and statistics: "consider the mass of figures and 'disgusting details' that I have before me, and have spared you, and be grateful . . . ."

Bowles reveled in the magnificent scenery and natural wonders of the West. He took special pleasure in conveying his excitement to his home-town subscribers, most of whom had never crossed the Hudson let alone the Mississippi. His first look at the Rockies left him breathless. They were "dream-like" and more beautiful than even the Swiss Alps he had visited earlier. The vistas he viewed "cleared the heart of earthly sorrow, and lead the soul up to its best and highest sources."[59] The air was exhilarating, air that was fresh, dry, clear, and strengthening. "No eastern mountain or ocean breeze," he maintained, "could match its enobling qualities."[60]

California's Yosemite Valley dazzled him. Indeed, the site left him speechless; he had difficulty finding words to put on paper. "As well interpret God in thirty-nine articles as portray it to you by word of mouth or pen." Yosemite, Bowles swore, "transcended marvelousness." It was "the confrontal of God face-to-face." Bowles spent a full four days worshipping the area.[61]

In early September of 1865, a big farewell party was held in honor of Colfax, Bross, Richardson, and Bowles. The banquet cost "no less than twenty-five dollars in gold," and was attended by two or three hundred of San Francisco's elite. The dinner was said to have been the best ever served in the town. Bowles enjoyed a new beverage—"beef-tea with just a smack of claret in it." He liked the taste and was especially pleased that it did not "make a wreck of his nerves the next day.[62]

Bowles came home by steamship via Panama. Much to his chagrin, the ocean voyage was rather unlike his earlier trans-Atlantic experience. To Europe he travelled with several hundred people, all pretty much upper class like himself. This time over a thousand people were on board. Only half were first or second class passengers; the rest were confined to steerage. The first two classes shared most of the same privileges. The major distinction were the meals; the first class dined at four, the second at one. Both classes had common interests and mingled freely throughout the journey. The ship's density displeased Bowles. "We are as thick as flies in August," he wrote. Bowles was put off by the lack of privacy. Bowles, a chronic insomniac, had great problems sleeping, because of all the babies on the ship, "at least one hundred of them . . . . New and kinder notions of old baby slaughtering King Herod prevailed among suffering passengers."[63]

As the ship continued southward, the weather became increasingly hot and humid. Decks and cabin floors were laden with bodies, asleep and half-asleep. Bowles felt the tropical languor come over him. All work, he observed, ceased. "A creamy hazy feeling possesses the senses—reading becomes an effort; cardplaying ceases to lure; dreaming, dozing, and scandal—talking grows to be the occupation of the ship's company." Bowles was disgusted by the prostitutes who plied their trade and he condemned the weak men who lacked self control.[64]

After a week's travel, the ship stopped in Acapulco, Mexico. The Mexican people failed to impress him; he thought them lazy and stupid. The women who sold fruits and vegetables were "gross . . . and dreary old hags."[65] Acapulco, Bowles wrote, was a backward town; there wasn't even a single road into the interior. The most sophisticated vehicle these primitive people had, Bowles huffed, was a wheelbarrow. He asked plaintively, "What can be done for a people who, with two hundred years and more of contact with civilization, can do no more for themselves?"[66]

Back at sea, Bowles and his shipmates soon arrived in Panama. He took a "long and crowded passenger train" across the fifty mile long isthmus. The ride was a "rare revelation" as he was awed by the abundance and variety of plant life. The leaves were so big and thick that he now knew "why Adam and Eve needed no tailor."[67]

The steamship on the Atlantic side was new and elegant. There was still discomfort—the ship was smaller than the one on the Pacific side—but the weather was better and everyone was in better spirits. The trip northward took exactly three weeks. Bowles was overjoyed to be back in the United States. New York City, where the ship docked, never looked better to him. A few days later, he arrived in Springfield.[68]

Bowles spent much of the fall making revisions in his published letters. The changes were not substantive. He liked the word "aboundingness" and left it in print, even though he was not sure if it was right. His close friend Charles Allen helped him. Bowles had some doubts—not voiced to anyone else—about his grammar and syntax. He admitted that his only guide was his ear and habit. For *Across the Continent*, Bowles added eight supplementary papers on topics as diverse as mines and Mormons.[69]

Bowles promoted his book with a vengeance. In a *Republican* ad, he called it "The Book of the Season." He noted that the *New York Times* had written that his letters were "The Ablest and Most Valuable Report ever Made of the Characteristics of the Western and Pacific Portions of our Union."[70] In a column, "Latest Advice from Santa Claus," it was noted that the book made the perfect Christmas present.[71] A subsequent January issue carried two entire columns of praise.[72] Meanwhile, the seasoned editor turned his attention to the battles being fought not on the battlefield, but in Congress. Recon-

Across the Continent:

A Stage Ride Over the Plains,

TO THE

ROCKY MOUNTAINS, THE MORMONS, AND THE PACIFIC STATES,

IN THE SUMMER OF 1865,

WITH SPEAKER COLFAX.

By SAMUEL BOWLES,

EDITOR OF THE SPRINGFIELD (MASS.) REPUBLICAN.

NEW EDITION.

SPRINGFIELD, MASS.:
SAMUEL BOWLES & COMPANY.
NEW YORK:
HURD & HOUGHTON.
1869.

structing the union was proving no easy task.

NOTES

1. *S.R.*, May 8, 1862, p. 2, col. II.

2. Merriam, I:364.

3. Ibid., pp. 366-367. Mary Bowles loved flowers, trees, and nature and was a member of the local horticultural society. See obituary of Mrs. Bowles, December 23, 1889, in scrapbooks, Springfield Library Local History Room.

4. Ibid., p. 369. Benjamin, or "Frank" as he was often called, did not write as many reports to the *Republican* as he was supposed to, and his older brother expressed disappointment.

5. *S.R.*, May 17, 1862, p. 4, col. III. One day's stay in Wales was enough for Bowles to confidently characterize the Welsh as "simple, sturdy, industrious, virtuous, and handsome."

6. Ibid., July 12, 1862, p. 2, col. III. Bowles refused to make friends with the English because they were, he believed, Confederate sympathizers. See Bowles to Anna Dickinson, April 1, 1871, Dickinson Papers, Library of Congress, Washington, D.C.

7. Merriam, I:369. On occasion, Bowles walked ten miles.

8. *S.R.*, June 21, 1862, p. 4, col. III.

9. Ibid., July 28, 1862, p. 2, col. III.

10. Merriam, I:385.

11. Ibid., p. 372.

12. Ibid., p. 384 and pp. 374-375.

13. Ibid., p. 378-379.

14. Ibid., p. 384.

15. Hooker, p. 88. The price of the paper also increased one hundred percent—from two to four cents.

16. *S.R.*, May 7, 1863, p. 2, col. I.

17. Ibid., September 9, 1863, p. 4, col. I. Bowles used his name to endorse products in his newspaper such as Stewarts new "Cook Stove." See *S.R.*, October 7, 1863, p. 7, col. I.

18. Edward Morin, "Springfield During the Civil War Years, 1861-1865," *Historical Journal of Western Massachusetts* (Fall 1974), p. 35.

19. Frisch, pp. 75-76 and Patricia Leal, "Springfield: Meeting the Challenge of the Civil War," May 8, 1975, Local History Room, Springfield City Library.

20. G. B. Prescott, "The U.S. Armory at Springfield," *Atlantic Monthly* (October 1863), p. 436.

21. Hooker, p. 88.

22. Frisch, p. 86.

23. Bowles to Dawes, February 26, 1861, in Merriam, I:318.

24. *S.R.*, February 6, 1865, p. 2, col. II.

25. John Mitchell, *Springfield, Massachusetts and the Coming of the Civil War*, Ph.D. dissertation, Boston University, 1960, p. 141.

26. Bowles to Franklin B. Sanborn, February 16, 1863, in Merriam, I:393.

27. Hooker, p. 96.

28. Bowles to Miss Maria Whitney, February 1, 1865, in Merriam, I:415.

29. David M. Potter, *Division and the Stresses of Reunion* (Glenview, Illinois: Scott, Foresman, 1973), p. 142.

30. Mitchell, p. 228.

31. Merriam, II:1-2.

32. Samuel Bowles, *Across the Continent* (Springfield: Samuel Bowles and Company, 1865), foreword.

33. Ibid., p. v.

34. Ibid., p. 6.

35. Ibid., pp. 45-49.

36. Frederick Merk, *Manifest Destiny and Mission in American History* (New York: Knopf, 1963). Bowles believed, for example, that Canada was destined to become part of the United States. See Bowles, p. 208.

37. Bowles, p. 8.

38. Ibid., pp. 366-367.

39. Ibid., p. 70.

40. Ibid., p. 8.

41. Ibid. p. 69.

42. Ibid., pp. 79-80.

43. Ibid., p. 86.

44. Ibid., p. 87.

45. Ibid., p. 99. Scrofula is a type of tuberculosis.

46. Ibid., pp. 123 and 107.

47. Ibid., p. 115.

48. Ibid., p. 116.

49. Ibid., p. 159. Surprisingly, Bowles' health held up pretty well along the way; although he was looking forward to getting some uninterrupted sleep in a comfortable bed and not in the corner of a "mud wagon." See Bowles, p. 213.

50. Ibid., p. 242.

51. Ibid., p. 239.

52. Ibid., p. 245.

53. Dinner Invitation, August 15, 1865 in Bowles Papers. The companies comprised the Chinese mercantile elite in California.

54. Bowles, pp. 250-254.

55. Ibid., pp. 273, 331-332.

56. Ibid., pp. 142-143.

57. Ibid., p. 348. Bowles speculated himself. He was president of the Boston and Chicago Gold Mining Company. His venture, apparently did not pan out. See Bowles to M. G. Clark, March 30, 1866, Bowles Papers. Bowles also bought some land outside Denver. Unfortunately, Denver grew the other way. See Hooker, p. 137.

58. Bowles, p. 312.

59. Ibid., p. 33.

60. Ibid., p. 140.

61. Ibid., pp. 223-224.

62. Ibid., p. 361.

63. Ibid., pp. 370-372.

64. Ibid., pp. 373-374.

65. Ibid., p. 375.

66. Ibid., p. 376.

67. Ibid., p. 382.

68. Ibid., p. 386. Surprisingly, in view of his fragile health, he suffered no substantive health problems in his four month sojourn.

69. Bowles to Charles Allen, November 23, 1865, in Merriam, II:46.

70. S.R., December 9, 1865, p. 5, col. VI.

71. Ibid., December 23, 1865, p. 4, col. V.

72. Ibid., January 31, 1866, p. 8, col. I.

CHAPTER V

COMBATING CORRUPTION

What was to become of post-war America? A nation divided for four bloody years awaited reconciliation. But how, and on whose terms? Should the southern states be treated as "conquered provinces" and administered by the strong hand of the federal government? Or had the Confederate states technically never left the union and, therefore, retained all the rights and privileges they enjoyed—except slavery—as before the war? The questions were many; the solution difficult. Bowles offered one solution to perhaps the thorniest problem, suffrage. He advocated a constitutional amendment that would have given all adults, including blacks and women, the franchise. Only illiterates would be disqualified.[1]

In early 1866, he left Springfield for Washington to promote his proposal and to report first-hand on the bitter squabble between the Congress and President Andrew Johnson. The Republican-controlled House and Senate and former Democrat Johnson were at loggerheads over the direction of reconstruction. It upset Bowles that Republican congressional leaders were "gloating" over their differences with Johnson. Bowles thought that unlike Lincoln, the Tennessean was too "thin-skinned." The immediate prospect, he wrote in February, was for contentious clashes, with no firm resolution in sight.[2] He blamed Johnson, but especially Congress for utterly failing "in dealing with the questions of reconstruction."[3] Later, he more often than not sided with the Congress. He was dismayed by Johnson's increasingly erratic behavior and he approved the Tenure-of-Office Act which prohibited a president from removing without Senate approval, any official whose senatorial confirmation was mandatory.[4] Bowles supported Johnson's impeachment and he was chagrined when Johnson was acquitted by a one-vote margin. "He was guilty. He deserved conviction. The nation needed it," Bowles wrote firmly.[5] Nevertheless, he refused to take part in the vituperation that fell upon the seven Republican Senators who courageously voted for acquittal.[6]

Meanwhile, that spring, Bowles received one of the great honors of his life. He was named a trustee of Amherst College replacing former Congressman and *Republican* editorial writer William B. Calhoun.[7] Over the years, Bowles had written flattering accounts of Amherst College commencements. His appointment was promoted by his friend Austin Dickinson and his father, former Congressman Edward Dickinson. Bowles' attendance at board meetings was spotty— he was often out of town—but his enthusiasm was great. Bowles supported Amherst's traditional emphasis on "classical education," but also advocated more electives, non-classical courses, and co-education.[8]

In October 1866, he was on the road again, this time heading for the coal fields of Pennsylvania. The trip's ostensible purpose was to study tax policy. Accompanying Bowles were several congressmen and Hugh McCullough, Secretary of the Treasury. As usual, Bowles wrote a series of letters to the *Republican*. He was struck by the sharp contrasts of the Keystone State. In Schuylkill at the height of the fall foliage, he was captivated by the colors and their "rich, intoxicating mass of glow. It was one long delirium of beauty, filling up and choking the soul of sense; another and sweeter and subtler shape of that fullness and ripeness and tropical reverie of sense that comes with hasheesh . . . ."[9]

If that was heaven, then hell took another form—Pittsburgh. The city was ugly, dirty, and noisy. Air saturated with soot made breathing difficult. The sun was barely able "to penetrate the gloom," Bowles reported, much before 10 o'clock, and then it had but "a sickly, faint glow." "A sensitive sinner," Bowles added, "on first arriving in Pittsburgh, [might] imagine himself within the very vestibule of his satanic majesty's dominions, and tremblingly lisp the unaccustomed prayer accordingly."[10]

Bowles stopped briefly in Philadelphia. He had always liked "the city of brotherly love," and he had some old acquaintances there. In one conversation, Bowles compared Philadelphia with its eastern rivals, New York and Boston. His guest informed the inquisitive editor that the differences among the cities were as follows: "In Boston, the question is 'What does he know?;' in New York, it's 'How much is he worth?;' and in Philadelphia, it's 'Who was his father?'"[11]

Bowles wrote little on the tax issue. He knew what interested his readers, and, more importantly, what bored them. He dreaded the prospect that the *Republican* be characterized as dull or lifeless. What he did write on the subject was a call for reforming the currency, and a temporary addition to taxes on imports.[12]

In 1867, Bowles' poor health burdened him once again. Mary also suffered through much of the year with her asthma and with a variety of other "female complaints." Bowles stayed in Springfield for the most part, concentrating on the business side of his newspaper operation. In the winter of 1867, the *Republican* moved into new headquarters. The change was necessitated by the paper's growth. The new building, on Main Street, had four floors with "a high basement story." The fourth floor housed the editorial rooms. Bowles' office was centrally located in the middle with easy access from all other rooms. Each floor had its own water closet.[13]

Samuel Bowles and Company was a lot more than just a newspaper. The firm did electrotyping and bookkeeping, in addition to printing sheet music, missing numbers, bronze printing, poster printing, and blank books.[14] The usually ailing editor had more than enough work supervising every detail of his *Republican*. Supervising every detail of the rest of his operation only wore him out further.

Later that year, the newspaper expanded once again to a double-sheet (eight pages) schedule three times a week, Monday, Wednesday, and Saturday. Bowles reminded his readers that at three cents a copy, the *Republican* was Springfield's best bargain. He appealed to his readers' thrift by pointing out to them that the Boston and New York newspapers were four or five cents an issue.[15] Meanwhile, Bowles enlarged the *Republican's* staff. Franklin Sanborn, who had been an occasional contributor, came on board as a regular editorial writer. General Francis Walker, with a special expertise in political economy, joined the staff, as did able junior assistants, Charles G. Whiting and Wilmot L. Warren.[16] Warren recalled that Bowles was often severe, and, indeed, even cruel. Yet, at the same time, "a word of approval from 'the chief,' coupled with one of his wonderful smiles was worth a hundred flatteries besides."[17]

On a typical work day, Bowles came into his office in a brusque, no-nonsense manner. He often said good-morning to no one. Months might go by before he spoke a word or two to a new employee. One neophyte was whistling while working at his desk. Bowles told him, "You needn't think you're doing that work very well." The chastened employee didn't whistle again for another week. A man who had trouble getting to work on time found on his desk a terse message: "Good-night at ten, sharp. Good-morning at nine, sharp." Handed an article that was sloppy or poorly thought out, Bowles would tear it up on the spot, and dictate what he wanted said.[18] Pity the poor man who made the same mistake twice.[19] One day, a staff member, speaking to the chief at home, asked him frankly, "Why do you sometimes go round among us silent and black as a thundercloud?" "I tell you," he answered, "there are times when the greatest kindness I can do my friends is to keep silent toward them." All the *Republican* employees knew the great physical strain Bowles was under and most reconciled themselves to the fact that it would probably never change.

Actually, even when Bowles was feeling well, his office demeanor was not that different. As a perfectionist, he expected only slightly less from others than he did of himself. As one of his secretaries noted, "The effect of his personality on his workers was to keep them under a strain . . . . He always kept the office shaken up . . . ." She also recalled, however, another side. Once Bowles invited six out-of-towners to dinner at his Central Street home. On the appointed day, he came into the office and was quite surprised that he had not received any replies. He telegraphed the guests and discovered that none of them had gotten an invitation. That evening the secretary found the invitations in her coat pocket, obviously unmailed. After a sleepless night, she confessed to Bowles. "He took it with perfect amiability, and not a word or look of reproof."[20]

Poor physical health plagued Bowles once again the next year. "It seemed," he wrote, "as if the bottom was falling out." Once again, he sought refuge in the west. In the late summer of 1868, he joined Speaker Colfax and Illinois Lieutenant Governor Bross on a trip to Colorado. Bowles' eldest daughter Sally accompanied her father. The party of about a dozen was led by the famed geologist-explorer Professor John Wesley Powell. Bowles hoped to repeat his earlier literary success and he wrote another series of letters to the *Republican*. They were in turn revised and compiled in his second book, *The Switzerland of America*.[21]

The trip was similar in many ways to his previous one. Bowles' articles focused on the scenery and topography of the land along with the folkways and mores of the people living in America's Switzerland, Colorado. He entertained his readers with several vivid sketches of the "off-beat" characters he encountered. Bowles contrasted the luxury of the train that took the party "to the end of the open road," with the horrific border town, Benton, Michigan. Benton, Bowles wrote, was not inaptly called "Hell on Wheels." "It was by day disgusting and by night dangerous; almost everybody was dirty, most filthy, and with the marks of lowest vice." He was especially outraged by "the hurdy-gurdy dancing and the vilest of sexual commerce," and he did his best to shield his eighteen year-old daughter from the immoral sights.[22]

Bowles survived his first night on the stagecoach, but just barely. "The air gets cold," he said, "the road grows dusty and chokes . . . the legs become stiff and numb, the temper edges, everybody is overcome with sleep, but can't stay asleep . . . the girls screech, the profane swear; some lady wants a smelling bottle . . . and her bag is somewhere on the floor,—nobody knows where—but found it must be; everybody's back hair comes down, and what is nature and what is art in costume and character is revealed . . . ."[23]

Bowles rode a mule for the first time. He asked his readers if they had ever ridden one. Mules had brains but were so obstinate! It took practically an eternity, Bowles continued, to get an idea registered. But when one finally does, the effect is overpowering. Then the mule forgets, and you're back to square one! His experience rendered a new faith in the transmigration of souls: "I know so many people who must have been mules once, or will be . . . ." Bowles remarked that he and his mule, "often had serious discussions—sometimes with sticks—but he generally got the best of the argument."[24]

The scenic highlight was Gray's Peak, the highest point in the Colorado Rockies. It was an arduous trek upward; but the reward made the toil well worth it. Bowles ranked Gray's Peak with the three or four greatest natural wonders of the world. "No Swiss mountain view carries such majestic sweep of distance . . . such uplifting into the presence of God; such dwarfing of the mortal sense, such welcome to the immortal thought . . . it was not man but God, that was about, before, in us."[25]

Bowles experienced the scare of his life in Colorado—"An Indian Scare." A breathless messenger rode into camp and warned Bowles and the company that he had met hostile Indians that very morning. They had pursued and shot at him, bullet holes piercing his saddle. The messenger exclaimed that he had escaped only by the fastest of riding and that the cut-throat Indians were only a few miles back and right on their trail. Fear and terror struck the party. "Every ear stretched for unaccustomed sound, every heart beat anxiously," Bowles reported. How did Bowles react to the danger? He confessed he "had the soundest, sweetest night's sleep he had had in the mountains." The next morning the party learned they were victims of a "villainous sensationalist." It was all a practical joke; a rather successful one.[26]

Bowles expatiated on Indian policy; he called for reform. The Indian problem, he wrote, should be the responsibility of a single agency in Washington and not divided between the Interior and War Departments. He argued that it was foolish to continue making treaties with the various tribes and that it was insane to put the Indians on par with the white man. "We know they are not our equals; we know that our right to the soil, as a race capable of its superior improvement is above theirs . . . ." Bowles pointed out that the higher race of white people had the God-given right to the land. He also agreed that the Indians should be kept from starving to death if at all possible. But, he concluded, "in all likelihood, it was the Indians' destiny to die."[27]

In late September 1868, Bowles returned to Springfield, "his health much improved by his open-air life in the mountains."[28] Meanwhile, before his trip to Colorado, Bowles had covered both the Democratic and Republican National Conventions that met in Chicago and New York respectively. Bowles ardently backed the Republican nominee for president, Ulysses S. Grant. He was even more enthusiastic about Grant's running mate, Speaker of the House, travelling companion and friend, Schuyler Colfax.[29] Grant defeated the Democratic nominee, Horatio Seymour, rather handily in the electoral college, but by a surprisingly narrow margin in the popular vote.

Bowles was deeply troubled by the political atmosphere of post-war America. It seemed to him that too many politicians were seeking office primarily to enrich themselves, rather than working for the public good. He was upset about what he perceived to be a new alliance being formed between politicians at all levels—Federal, state, and municipal—and a new breed of businessmen who worshipped at the shrine of gold and carried themselves with a less than dignified deportment. The personification of his fears was a fellow New Englander, James Fisk, Jr.

Fisk had worked his way up from a small town peddler in Brattleboro, Vermont (which borders Massachusetts and was well within the *Republican* delivery territory) to, along with his partner, James Gould, head of the Erie Railway. They used its stock, in a complicated illegal scheme to bilk other share-holders and speculators in the company. Fisk and Gould made a small fortune.[30] Fisk's maneuverings infuriated Bowles, who was also sickened by the coarse behavior of the man, who, Bowles wrote, "was almost as broad as he is high, and so round that he rolls rather than walks." Bowles charged in a *Republican* editorial that Fisk was a swindler. He claimed that Fisk and his associates seemed to "own" at least several New York courts. Bowles concluded by citing some of Fisk's friends who predicted that he would wind up in a state prison or a lunatic asylum, where Fisk's father was presumably housed.[31]

Fisk promptly responded with a libel suit against the *Republican* for $50,000. His suit, originally filed in Massachusetts, was withdrawn and presented in a New York court.[32] Bowles' response was hardly one of fear. He mocked the rotund rascal in a sarcastic column entitled "Our Friend Mr. James Fisk Jr." Bowles was saddened that his earlier column on Fisk did not result in a letter of thanks or a few thousand shares of Erie stock. He fancied hearing Fisk's "rich round voice shouting down the page to the printer to grind off another half million of stock or bonds—whatever form happens to be on the press—for that clever Republican fellow up in Springfield,—bless his heart." Bowles closed by writing that Fisk must be insane already; after all "he don't recognize his friends."[33] Fisk fumed and plotted his revenge. Little did the unsuspecting Bowles know what was in store for him on a social visit to New York City later in the month.

On December 23, at about 8:00 p.m., Bowles was meeting at the elegant Fifth Avenue Hotel with Murat Halstead, editor of the *Cincinnati Commercial*, and William Bond, president of the New Almaden Quicksilver Company. The lobby was packed with the city's elite. Without a warning, a deputy sheriff appeared, stood alongside Bowles, and politely but firmly told the startled editor that he carried orders for his immediate arrest. Stunned, Bowles made only one request, that he be permitted to cross the street to the Albermarle Hotel to inform his ailing wife. His request was denied. A carriage was waiting at the hotel's main entrance as Bowles was quickly whisked outside. The deputy sheriff blared at the coachman, "Drive to Ludlow Street and be in a d–d hurry too." Word spread quickly "throughout the famous resorts in the vicinity of Madison Square" as a throng of people quickly descended to the jail.

The dazed editor was first taken to a well-appointed sitting room where he was interrogated by the Deputy Warden in charge:

"Deputy Warden: I suppose you are not accustomed to jail life?
Bowles: Not particularly so. I am about receiving my first experience.
Deputy Warden: Well I guess it won't be very rough for you. We don't usually handle gentlemen very roughly here, particularly when they are brought in on civil writs. Yours is a civil case I believe?
Bowles: It strikes me as decidedly uncivil.
Deputy Warden: Ah, yes; very good. Ha ha ha! That's tip top."

The warden asked Bowles if he was hungry and would like something to eat. Bowles declined. He was told that a nice room, right off the dining area was reserved in his honor. Bowles pleaded with the warden to send one of his subordinates back up Fifth Avenue to tell Mrs. Bowles what was happening. The warden refused, but he let a representative of the crowd that had gathered outside come in and talk briefly. Halstead, the group's spokesman, demanded that Bowles be released at once. He was told that was impossible. It was too late—10.00 p.m.—Bowles would have to spend the night in jail. Halstead left, but not without first slipping Bowles a note letting him know that Mary was alright.

Halstead, with some other of Bowles' friends, quickly drove to a reception for the mayor-elect, A. Oakey Hall, where the city sheriff, Judge McCunn (who issued the order of arrest), and big Jim Fisk were present. Halstead again demanded Bowles' immediate release. Halstead was turned down. At the jail, Bowles read newspapers well into the night and then asked to go to sleep. His stark cell was ten by fifteen feet with a small window opening. The cell was next to an alley that separated the jail from the Essex Street Market. The next morning, Mrs. Bowles went to a prominent attorney, Clarence A. Seward, who prepared the necessary legal papers to free her husband wih a $50,000 bond.[34] Bowles paid $17.50 for room and an "excellent breakfast of tea and toast" and was let go just before noon.[35]

The *Republican* voiced its indignation the next day. It charged that Bowles was set-up and purposely arrested at night so he would be forced to spend an evening in jail. It thundered, incorrectly, that the actions of the officers were "violent and ungentlemanly."[36] Bowles, however, took his incarceration philosophically. He was reminded of a sagacious Frenchman who wrote that "Experience was all that life could give us, and that whosoever offered a fresh bit of that was a real if unconscious philanthropist."[37]

The Bowles returned home immediately. Christmas eve was no time to be away from family, and besides they were expecting guests—Vice President-elect Colfax and his wife.[38] Bowles luxuriated in his new role as hero. His dramatic episode in New York was splashed across the front page in many of the nation's newspapers. Editorial opinion overwhelmingly supported Bowles and lashed out at what Secretary of the Navy Gideon Welles wrote in his dairy was the "sorry exhibition of petty spite on the part of Fisk."[39]

Several days later, Bowles received a letter from Alexander Bullock, representing Massachusetts' political elite, requesting his presence at a dinner in his honor testifying to their respect for his course as an "independent editor."[40] Bowles was touched, but he promptly replied that although he accepted the compliment with "gratitude and pride," he was unable to accept the invitation. Bowles explained that to accept would compromise his position of independent journalism, which he would never allow to happen.[41]

As it turned out, Bowles was not finished with Fisk and his entourage. The *Republican* continued to focus its attention on the "Erie Speculators," the Tweed ring, and the "bought off" judges of New York. In late 1870, the *Republican's* New York correspondent wrote the following words about Fisk's counsel David Dudley Field: "His receipts as counsel for the Erie railroad company alone are understood to have exceeded $200,000 in a single year, and his regular income is enormous. His connection with Fisk and Gould secures him the favor of Barnard and other ring judges, though it has destroyed his reputation as a high-toned lawyer with the public."[42]

Field was one of New York's most prominent lawyers. Along with his son, Dudley Field, he had been employed by the Erie directors to protect their interests and to battle adversaries in court. Both Fields took umbrage at the criticism directed at them by Bowles' reporter. They wrote Bowles seeking a retraction or an apology.[43] Bowles' reply, however, justified and reinforced the sentiments of his New York correspondent. Thus began a series of twenty letters between the Fields and Bowles on the role of lawyers and the press in a free society. Eventually they were put into pamphlet form, the Fields' version, expurgated, and Bowles' version, complete. The letters attracted wide attention in the professions.[44]

Bowles said that, although he did not like the attack on Field's character, he agreed with the sentiment that "among your old friends in Western Massachusetts . . . [there is] mingled sorrow and indignation at your professional associations with Fisk and Gould and their desperate schemes."[45] Bowles shortly thereafter received an indignant letter from the younger Field informing him that they had helped him get out of jail and were never thanked. Furthermore, Field continued, his father was not "mean" or "avaristic" and they never got anywhere near $200,000 from the Erie Railway.[46]

Bowles thanked the Fields for getting him out of jail and wrote that he had only found out about that a little while earlier. He assured them that he had only sought their aid for his wife's sake. Bowles reiterated his contention that their association with Fisk was a disgrace, and he closed by writing that he was "credibly informed" that on the morning after his arrest, the son had said "that it was a disgrace to the family to have such a client as Fisk."[47]

The elder Field quickly responded. He argued forcefully that Bowles had no right to render "judgement" upon him. He told Bowles that he should only publish the facts and not opinions about the personality or behavior of private citizens. Field argued that he had the right to represent Gould and Fisk, indeed, that he was "bound to." "Everyone," Field wrote, "deserves legal aid."[48]

Bowles replied, "The gathering and publication of *facts* is but one part of its [journalism's] vocation. To express *opinions* is a higher and larger share of its duties. The conduct of public men before the public is the legitimate subject of its discussion." Bowles scoffed at the notion that a lawyer was not a public man. The irritated editor claimed that he had had to "walk backward with averted eyes through much of the history of your professional association with those notorious clients that have dragged down your professional fame." Bowles concluded that he was happy that Field was satisfied with the propriety of his conduct, but that if he was right, then his friends, his profession, and the public must be wrong.[49]

Field angrily restated his point that all men, even bad men, need and have a right to legal counsel. Bowles' "backward with averted eyes" statement struck a raw nerve in the barrister. Field called Bowles an "effete" and "sentimental school girl." He insisted that public opinion was totally irrelevant to their controversy and again informed Bowles that he had done nothing illegal.[50]

Bowles shot back that he had never accused Field of doing anything illegal. The question, Bowles insisted, was one of "broad public morality." He charged that Field had offended "the moral sense of the public" and he stated self-righteously that a man *should* suffer for his bad character.[51]

The younger Field re-entered the war of words by charging that Bowles had failed to retract what he knew were false assertions. He vehemently denied ever having told his father that it was a disgrace having Fisk as a client. He added that even if Fisk's father was a lunatic, the *Republican* had no right to print it. He closed by reminding Bowles that he had contradicted himself when he wrote that he did not attack the elder Field more sharply owing to "personal relations." But is it not, he reminded Bowles, "the duty of a journalist to tell the truth regardless of personal feelings?"[52]

As much as it pained him to admit it, Bowles agreed that Field had a point. "You are right, my duty as a journalist should not have been sacrificed to personal considerations." Bowles then, more comfortably, took the offensive. He contended that there was a "natural and legitimate demand" for information about the Fisk family history. He said his source for the remark about the disgrace of having Fisk as a client came "almost directly from a distinguished member of your family." He averred that even if their fee was not $200,000, then $175,000 was still an enormous amount of money.

Bowles finished the letter by concluding that their correspondence was about at an end, and he thanked the Fields for their services the night their "distinguished client clapped me in jail."[53]

But the duel by letter was not over. The senior Field called Bowles a libeler and said that Bowles' reply to his son's letter was a disgrace and not fit to print.[54] The angered Bowles replied that if the letter was such a "'disgrace,' then why didn't you print it since it could only have injured me and my cause."[55]

Five more letters passed between the two parties, as each sought the last word. Field asked Bowles if he thought himself "the self-proclaimed spokesman for the Public Conscience?"[56] Bowles charged that Field was "wantonly reckless of the truth."[57]

On January 30, 1871, in an unprecedented issue of the *Republican*, Bowles printed the entire correspondence between the two principles. The contents filled all of pages one and two and nearly the entire third page. He taunted Field for suppressing two letters, and he summarized his main points for those not willing to read the transcript in its entirety. He advised Field and his cohorts to familiarize themselves with the Ten Commandments.[58] Bowles' final thought on Field came six years later. Writing to President Rutherford B. Hayes, he repeated a remark made by one of "the Adams' boys," that "Field had a great reputation in England because he was supposed to be the leading lawyer of America, and that he was thought to be a great lawyer in America because he had such an English reputation."[59]

NOTES

1. Merriam, II:20.

2. *S.R.*, February 26, 1866, p. 2, col. II.

3. Ibid., February 28, 1866, p. 1, col. III.

4.   Merriam, II:33.

5.   Ibid., p. 36.

6.   Ibid., p. 37.

7.   *S.R.*, April 21, 1866, p. 2, col. I. Bowles' appointment was approved by the state legislature. At that time, the state legislature approved trustees for colleges. Bowles missed many trustee meetings, which he regretted, but it could not be helped as he was so often out of town. Undoubtedly, what was more important to the college was his power and influence in Massachusetts and with the governor and legislature.

8.   Merriam, II:80. Over one hundred years later, Amherst College finally took Bowles' advice and admitted women. Bowles also advocated the merger of Amherst and Williams College to make it the equal of a Yale or Harvard.

9.   Ibid., p. 52. Whether Bowles used hasheesh or not is problematic. Certainly with all his pain and suffering, it is possible.

10.   *S.R.*, November 21, 1866, p. 1, col. I.

11.   Ibid., October 31, 1866, p. 1, col. I. See also Edward Digby Baltzell, *Puritan Boston and Quaker Philadelphia* (Boston: Beacon Press, 1979).

12.   Merriam, II:53.

13.   *S.R.*, February 9, 1867, p. 1, col. I.

14.   Ibid., February 23, 1867, p. 2, col. IV.

15.   Ibid., October 28, 1867, p. 4, col. I. Improved rail service brought the Boston and New York papers more quickly to Springfield, making them even more competitive.

16.   Merriam, II:68.

17.   Ibid., p. 69.

18.   Ibid., pp. 69-70.

19.   Ibid., p. 72. For example, Bowles would get very upset at staff who capitalized too often. An old saying at the paper was that "Only Jesus Christ and Samuel Bowles were capitalized at the *Republican*." See Griffin, p. 20.

20.   Merriam, II:71-72. Of course, it may not have been an important dinner; or perhaps it was one he was not looking forward to.

21. Ibid., p. 81. In 1869, Bowles condensed *Across the Continent* and *The Switzerland of America* into one book, *Our New West*. It sold 23,000 copies. Colfax's mind was not on business this trip. He "was too busy courting one of the unattached ladies of the group to pay much attention to anything else." See John Upton Terrel, *The Man Who Rediscovered America: A Biography of John Wesley Powell* (New York: Weybright and Talley, 1969), p. 61.

22. Samuel Bowles, *The Switzerland of America: Colorado, Its Parks and Mountains* (Springfield: Samuel Bowles and Company, 1868), pp. 21-22.

23. Ibid., p. 30.

24. Ibid., p. 57.

25. Ibid., p. 95.

26. Ibid., pp. 120-123.

27. Ibid., pp. 124-126.

28. *S.R.*, September 15, 1868, p. 2, col. I.

29. The previous year, however, Bowles backed Governor John A. Andrew of Massachusetts for the vice-presidency. See A. G. Browne, Jr. to Governor Andrew, October 22, 1867, in Andrew Papers, Massachusetts Historical Society.

30. Merriam, II:93.

31. *S.R.*, November 28, 1868, p. 4, col. I.

32. Merriam, II:94-95. The suit was later withdrawn.

33. *S.R.*, December 5, 1868, p. 4, col. II.

34. This account of Bowles' memorable experience is taken from the *New York Sun*, December 24, 1868, p. 1, col. I.

35. *S.R.*, December 28, 1868, p. 5, col. I.

36. Ibid., December 24, 1868, p. 2, col. IV.

37. Ibid., December 28, 1868, p. 5, col. I.

38. Ibid., December 24, 1868, p. 2, col. I. Colfax met the Bowles' with his new wife, Nellie Wade, whom he had courted on his Colorado trip. See Wallace Stegner, *Beyond the Hundredth Meridian: John Wesley Powell and the Second Opening of the West* (Boston: Houghton Mifflin, 1954), p. 31.

39. Howard K. Beale, editor, *Diary of Gideon Wells, Volume III* (New York: Norton, 1960), p. 490.

40. Alexander Bullock to Samuel Bowles, December 24, 1868, Bowles Papers. Several dozen other names appeared, representing a broad spectrum of the political and commercial leadership of the state.

41. *S.R.*, December 29, 1868, p. 2, col. IV.

42. Hooker, p. 108.

43. Samuel Bowles, *The Lawyer and His Clients: The Rights and Duties of Lawyers; the Rights and Duties of the Press; The Opinions of the Public* (Springfield: Samuel Bowles and Company, 1871), p. 1. Heretofore, Bowles' pamphlet.

44. Merriam, II:97-98.

45. David Dudley Field to Bowles, December 27, 1870 in Bowles' pamphlet, p. 1.

46. Dudley Field to Bowles, December 27, 1870, pp. 2-3, ibid.

47. Bowles to Dudley Field, December 29, 1870, pp. 4-5, ibid.

48. David Dudley Field to Bowles, December 30, 1870, pp. 5-6, ibid.

49. Bowles to David Dudley Field, January 3, 1871, pp. 6-8, ibid.

50. David Dudley Field to Bowles, January 5, 1871, pp. 8-9, ibid.

51. Bowles to David Dudley Field, January 10, 1871, p. 10, ibid.

52. Dudley Field to Bowles, January 9, 1871, pp. 10-12, ibid.

53. Bowles to Dudley Field, January 13, 1871, pp. 13-16, ibid.

54. David Dudley Field to Bowles, January 16, 1871, pp. 16-17, ibid.

55. Bowles to David Dudley Field, January 17, 1871, p. 17, ibid.

56. David Dudley Field to Bowles, January 27, 1871, p. 21, ibid.

57. Bowles to David Dudley Field, January 26, 1871, pp. 19-20, ibid.

58. Merriam, II:101.

59. Ibid., II:421.

CHAPTER VI

THE WOMEN

The battles against corruption and the Fields left Bowles frazzled. Late at night after work, he would drag his weary body up the Maple Street hill toward his comfortable Central Street home. Here he insisted on quiet. Even then, Bowles had difficulty falling asleep. He often tossed and turned and was still awake at sunrise. He often said, "I am hungry for sleep." In the morning, an eerie silence enveloped the house. The children knew that their father needed his rest badly, and Bowles was most appreciative with their compliance. He once said "The quiet of my home has lengthened my life."[1]

Bowles took great comfort in his family. He and Mary had seven children, the last born in 1868. Bowles was a kind and loving father, who by virtue of his incredible work schedule, however, did not spend much time with them. He saw to it that each of his children, when of age, was given responsibilities around the house. The eldest daughter had sundry chores inside the home. Another was in charge of supplies for the barn. But just like at the *Republican* office, Bowles often wound up taking over the responsibilities he had delegated.[2]

Mary Bowles suffered from frequent and often severe bouts of asthma. During one bad attack, while away in Washington, Bowles prescribed a ten-point plan to reduce her suffering by two-thirds. Among the tips were not to eat cake or pastry, never read an exciting book in the evening, and never go to the hall when the front door was open.[3] Throughout most of their married life, Mary needed and received outside help to maintain the house.[4] In this regard, no one person played a more important role in her life than Maria Whitney.

Aside from his wife, no other woman meant more to Samuel Bowles than Northampton's Maria Whitney. Whitney's role in the Bowles family was multi-dimensional. In 1860, when Bowles was recuperating at Dr. Denniston's "invalid house" in Northampton, she saw him practically every day. In addition, she stayed with Mrs. Bowles during many of her bouts of illness, earning the gratitude of Samuel. "I do not know what Mary would have done without her," he wrote. "She has been most sisterly, most valuable, and cemented a holy friendship among us all." Whitney accompanied the oldest Bowles children, Sallie and Samuel, when they attended school in Europe. Bowles went to see them twice. His other vacations sometimes coincided with Maria's and she often took part in family outings. With Bowles' help, she was appointed Instructor of French and German at the new Smith College.[5]

In 1862, Mrs. Bowles gave birth to her son Charles Allen, and she recuperated in New York City. Coincidentally, Maria Whitney was staying in the city at the same time. Whitney wrote her sister-in-law that Samuel Bowles came to visit her often and was a "most agreeable and delightful companion."[6] Later, she wrote her brother Will that Bowles visits on Sundays and when he does "I shall feel free to go off [with him] for all the times he stays."[7] In early 1864, Bowles was depressed because Whitney went off to California. "Her going has been a trial to me," he wrote Susan Dickinson, "but I should be unworthy the rich gift of her friendship did I allow it to blue my life . . . . Her gifts to me are too great and noble to be spoiled by such unworthiness."[8]

Maria's relationship with Bowles raised eyebrows. One skeptic was her brother William, noted professor of geology at Yale. She pleaded with him and his wife to understand her relationship with Bowles, and to give it their approval as best they could. She urged them not to begrudge her all the friendship she could get, and she asked for their trust.[9]

Mary Bowles reacted with mixed emotions. She liked Maria—her distant relative—and she certainly appreciated all that Maria had done for her and her family. Mary knew there were times when Maria would have preferred to leave the household, but stayed out of a sense of duty. Maria, in turn, viewed such occasions as an opportunity to prove the value of a friendship "that ought not to be neglected."[10] When Whitney was sick in Italy, Mary Bowles expressed sincere concern for her health and wished that she "could do more for her and that she loved me as I sometimes feel I love her when I think how much she is to those I love."[11]

Maria Whitney

Mary Bowles

Nevertheless, the friendship between her husband and her talented friend produced much tension. Rumors of an affair were inevitable when Bowles, a married man with seven children, and pretty, petite Maria were seen together on numerous occasions. There was talk, and some of it filtered back to Samuel Bowles' plain-looking and overweight wife. Word got back to Whitney from her sister-in-law Lizzie that Mrs. Bowles was saying "disloyal and unkind" things about her. Others had said that their friendship was a "forced one on Mrs. Bowles' part only tolerated to avoid further separation from her husband." Whitney confronted Mrs. Bowles who denied ever having made any unflattering remarks. Presumably, Whitney told Mary that she and Mr. Bowles were friends and nothing more.[12] Samuel Bowles would not give up Maria—whatever their relationship—under any circumstances and Mary had to live with that fact, like it or not. When Samuel and Mary Bowles left Springfield for New York City to see off their son and daughter to Europe, Mary was miffed when, instead of having Whitney meet them at the dock, she spent the entire day with them at the hotel.[13]

Samuel Bowles missed Maria Whitney when she was away. How was he, he asked her, to maintain his "physical well-being" and "sweetness of heart" under such circumstances?[14] In another letter to her, writing while depressed, he called their friendship "sacred."[15] He concluded another letter by wishing her love, "the appropriate sort."[16] Both trips to the continent that she accompanied the Bowles' children were paid for by the editor. She was acting in an official capacity as a tutor and guide, she explained to her dubious brother Will.[17]

Bowles was devoted to Maria Whitney and most probably did "love" her. There is no evidence, however, that their relationship had a physical dimension as well. Certainly there were ample opportunities. In any event, Bowles confided in her unlike any other person in his life. He discussed with the shy but erudite Whitney his hopes, fears, dreams, and desires. No one else, not even his wife, received a more complete view of his philosophy of life and his religious ideas. Didn't she agree, he asked, "how little great men can be—the larger the smaller?" Or, he wondered, was it only the contrast, the conspicuousness? He wanted to know what she thought of the proposition that "nature compensates for great gifts in one direction by withholding in others."[18] He discussed with her his views on immortality. In the next world—he had his doubts as to its existence—rest in its

84

highest sense would dominate. The laws in that other world would forbid "weariness and striving, and all that torments us here." He believed that "God there must be to us all that our dreams and ideals are here." The only people who were truly happy in life, he reckoned, were idiots.[19]

Bowles was highly opinionated on the question of the nature of the female. As a young man, he congratulated his friend on the birth of his son, glad it was not a girl. Girls are appendages, he thought, necessary ones perhaps, but still appendages.[20] Women, he was certain, were naturally more inquisitive than men.[21] Bowles observed that nothing made a woman happier than buying a new bonnet. And if she got it at a "bargain" price, well, Bowles figured it was about as near to heaven as "the ordinary feminine soul" could get.[22] As the years progressed, however, Bowles' views generally became more enlightened. In a frank letter to a female friend, he expounded on the topic. "The lamb," he wrote, "has been protected by the wolf long enough . . . . She should have care of herself; and so far as laws and social customs are concerned, men and women should come together on a platform of perfect equality."[23]

His fullest thoughts on the subject came in a long editorial in early 1870 entitled "The New Reform—Woman's Rights and Man's Rights—The Question Restated." Bowles wrote that Susan B. Anthony was not born "three hundred years ago." If she had been, the movement would have doubtless come on sooner. Women must, Bowles argued, be allowed to take a "larger and more independent share in all the duties and responsibilities of life." Bowles pointed out that modern life was becoming more complex and that the new employment opportunities of the day were as suited to women as to men. Bowles called for immediate legal action. He demanded that men and women, and husbands and wives, be given "equal responsibility to each other." He urged equality of property rights. Finally, he was a staunch supporter of women's suffrage. The ballot box, he wrote, "stands for position, stands for responsibility, [and] stands for power . . . and as such it is rightly put at the forefront of the women's movement. Women's advance would advance men too, and serve the cause of God."[24]

Bowles strongly believed in the benefits of marriage. He attributed much of his success to the fact that he married early. In 1870, a divorce in Massachusetts could only be granted on grounds of adultery or desertion for at least five years. To remarry, one had to obtain special permission from a court. A newly-proposed bill in the legislature shortened the desertion period by two years, and permitted remarriage by both parties without court approval. Bowles was adamantly opposed: "Single life should be the penalty for the mistake of wrong mating." Bowles believed there would have been a flood of divorce if the new bill was enacted. The harder it was to get a divorce, he reasoned, the more carefully and thoughtfully people would enter marriage. Indeed, not only was Bowles opposed to liberalizing the divorce statutes, he wanted to make it even more difficult to get a divorce. Yes, he confessed, some individuals would suffer, but more importantly, society would gain. Bowles was pleased that, despite House passage, the new divorce bill was quashed in the more conservative Senate.[25]

Bowles' belief in the sanctity of marriage was genuine. Yet throughout his married life, he enjoyed the company—often alone—of other pretty, bright, talented, and usually single women besides Maria Whitney. He treated women as intellectual equals and simultaneously "with a kind of chivalrous deference."[26] He was interested, however, in more than just their minds. He took a fancy to a Mrs. Catherine Scott Turner, a friend of Susan Dickinson. Bowles wrote Susan asking her if the recently-widowed Turner, who was visiting in Amherst, would like to see Northampton. Bowles offered to spend the day with the attractive widow, driving her about and showing her the sights.[27]

Bowles was a stickler for time. His subordinates were well aware of their boss' distaste for tardiness. Bowles did not like to keep his peers waiting either. Only an event of some importance would keep him from his appointed rounds . . . like a chance encounter with a young woman. In New York to meet with Whitelaw Reid, editor of the *New York Tribune*, Bowles was stopped near Reid's office by "an interesting young woman." In his letter of apology to Reid, he explained, "The result—the old story: Staid two hours and lunched and when I got out it was too late for any man."[28] Bowles, a very busy man, sometimes found the time to do favors for other men. He always found time, however, to help out a woman.[29] He was a veritable fountain of praise and encouragement to female writers.[30]

Bowles was enamoured with feminist Anna Dickinson.[31] Dickinson was a popular orator who spoke with a "fiery passion and remarkable vituperation."[32] When she apologized for asking for some of his valuable time, Bowles would hear nothing of it. "Why should you apologize for asking anything of me?" he wrote. "You have long ago earned the right to anything and everything that I could do for you."[33] Later he asked her to let him have the opportunity to serve her whenever his assistance was needed.[34] She took him up on his offer at least several times. When she expressed to Bowles her interest in a theatrical career on the continent, he promptly wrote a friend in Paris inquiring about "the opportunities for dramatic instruction . . . ."[35] When Dickinson's whereabouts were unknown, he wrote to her last address annoyingly asking what had become of her. Later he invited Dickinson to a birthday celebration held in his honor in New York and he eagerly anticipated her presence in her "best gown."[36] At another point, Bowles was disappointed when he had to cancel a planned New York visit, and thus he could not see the women he "loved," Kate Field and Anna Dickinson.[37] Afterwards, Bowles urged Dickinson to stop in and see him before taking an extended trip south. He wanted to speak to her face to face. He wrote that he was "not ashamed to say everything he thought and felt to her and that she needn't be ashamed to hear him."[38]

Women not in the Dickinson or Whitney mold held little interest for Bowles. On his first trip abroad, he confided to his friend Charles Allen that European women didn't fascinate him very much. He noted that it wasn't that difficult to be "virtuous." Bowles was not impressed with the "Contenental dames" of France and Germany. He admitted that the "demi-monde" had a certain beauty, but not for him. He liked his women "natural."[39] The women of San Francisco also offered little temptation to the visiting eastern editor. Bowles described them as "mannish, materialistic, fast, and loud." They were vain, weak, and unfaithful, he added. They reminded him of the Parisian demi-monde. Their extravagance, he noted, was known to all in the region. As a matter of fact, he wrote, and as amazing as it may seem, the quality of men, in great contrast to the east, was superior to that of women.[40]

Bowles thought a lot about women. He certainly enjoyed their company. He loved his wife, Maria Whitney, and, to a lesser extent, Anna Dickinson. But his two great passions in his life were his newspaper and politics. In 1872, they would become entwined as never before.

NOTES

1. Merriam, II:139.

2. Ibid., pp. 140-141.

3. Ibid., p. 169.

4. The Bowles advertised in the classified section of the *Republican*. One example was a request for "A first-class Cook, one who is also a good washer and ironer." See *S.R.*, March 3, 1866, p. 8, col. V.

5. Leyda, Vol. I, p. 1xxviii.

6. Maria Whitney to sister-in-law Elizabeth Whitney, early January 1862, in Leyda, Vol. II, pp. 44-45. Bowles told Maria Whitney that his wife was pregnant even though it was supposed to be a "profound secret."

7. Maria Whitney to brother Will, October 8, 1863, ibid., p. 83.

8. Samuel Bowles to Susan Dickinson, February 26, 1864, ibid., p. 86.

9. Maria Whitney to William Whitney, September 13, 1865, in Whitney Family Papers, Sterling Memorial Library, Yale University, New Haven.

10. Maria Whitney to William Whitney, February 23, 1867, ibid.

11. Mary Bowles to her son Samuel, March 25, 1871, in Leyda, Vol. II, p. 172.

12. Maria Whitney to Lizzie Whitney, March 10, 1868, ibid., p. 129.

13. Mary Bowles to her son Samuel, October 24, 1869, ibid., p. 142.

14. Merriam, II:148.

15. Ibid., p. 160.

16. Ibid., p. 165. Unfortunately, Whitney, who outlived Bowles by thirty-two years, "destroyed all her correspondence, as she wished to leave nothing to burden any relatives." See Sewall, p. 751.

17. Maria Whitney to brother Will, February 26, 1871, in Leyda, Vol. II, p. 170. Bowles also bought her books to read. The more books he could buy her, the happier he was. See Merriam, Vol. II, pp. 411 and 415.

18. Merriam, II:413.

19. Ibid., pp. 371-372.

20. Bowles to Henry Dawes, August 6, 1855, Dawes Papers.

21. Bowles to Anna Dickinson, April 1, 1871, Anna Dickinson Papers, Library of Congress, Washington, D.C.

22. Samuel Bowles to son Samuel, May 13, 1870, in Leyda, Vol. II, p. 148.

23. Merriam, II:336.

24. *S.R.*, February 14, 1870, p. 2, col. I and III. Bowles was a leader of the women's suffrage movement in Massachusetts. See *S.R.*, January 21, 1870, p. 4, col. IV.

25. Merriam, II:389-390.

26. Ibid., p. 409.

27. Samuel Bowles to Susan Dickinson, late October 1861, in Leyda, Vol. II, p. 37.

28. Bowles to Whitelaw Reid, February 17, 1871, in Whitelaw Reid Papers, Library of Congress, Washington, D.C.

29. Bowles to Reid, September 11, 1871, ibid. This favor was done for Kate Field, *New York Tribune* correspondent and former *Springfield Republican* writer. Field was a dynamic, attractive, single woman with many gentlemen admirers. See *Notable American Women*, Vol. I, edited by Edward James (Cambridge: Belknap Press of Harvard University Press, 1971), p. 614.

30. Bowles to Kate Field, January 6, 1874, in Reid Papers, and Merriam, II:333.

31. Anna Dickinson was not related to the Dickinsons of Amherst.

32, Robert McHenry, editor, *Liberty's Women* (Springfield: Merriam Webster, 1976), pp. 100-101.

33. Bowles to Anna Dickinson, April 1, 1871, Dickinson Papers.

34. Bowles to Dickinson, October 24, 1871, ibid.

35. Bowles to W. H. Huntington, October 24, 1871, ibid.

36. Bowles to Dickinson, January 30, 1874, ibid.

37. Bowles to James Brooks, November 19, 1874, ibid. Although he "loved" her, again it does not necessarily mean there was a sexual relationship.

The term "love" was used more liberally in such matters in nineteenth century America.

38. Bowles to Dickinson, September 1872, ibid. For more information on this fiercely independent woman who so attracted Bowles, see Giraud Chester, *Embattled Maiden: The Life of Anna Dickinson* (New York: Putnam, 1951). Five years later on January 29, 1877, he ended another letter, "with much love and a great desire to see you face to face."

39. Merriam, II:370.

40. Bowles, *Across the Continent*, p. 324. Bowles' comments on San Francisco's women created a storm of controversy. See Merriam, II:46, and 50.

CHAPTER VII

EIGHTEEN SEVENTY–TWO: "DEVOID OF HISTORY"

Eighteeen seventy-two started off well enough for the tiring forty-six year old editor. He journeyed west once again and wrote a short series of articles to the *Republican* entitled "A WINTER TRIP WEST." He liked St. Louis and predicted it would become "the great city of the whole Mississippi Valley region."[1] The next week in Colorado, he praised its "salubrious climate." Colorado was the perfect place for people in failing health. It was a haven for dyspeptics and those in the early stages of lung difficulty, wrote Bowles, who happened to suffer from both ailments.[2] Bowles closed his letters commenting favorably on the burgeoning stock raising and wool growing business of the region.[3]

Bowles' newspaper was enjoying great success. Circulation of the daily *Springfield Republican* surpassed the ten thousand mark in early 1872 and sales of the weekly *Republican* were greater by thousands. Bowles proudly announced the purchase of a new Four Cylinder Rotary Hoe which improved production dramatically. The machine cost $25,000. Unfortunately, Bowles wrote, the new realities of newspaper publishing required extensive night work. Bowles refused to print the *Republican* until all the telegraph dispatches were in. The dispatches never ended by 2 a.m. and frequently continued until 4 a.m. Bowles was determined to have the paper distributed in town by 6 a.m. and on the earliest trains out of town. The fresher the newspaper, the better the sales.[4]

As the circulation rose in early 1872, so did Bowles' blood pressure. He was boiling mad over the direction that the Republican Party, the party that he had helped to found, had taken in recent years. An enthusiastic Grant supporter in 1868, Bowles had become outraged at administration policies on both foreign and domestic fronts. Grant's first term, thought Bowles and like-minded Republicans, was characterized by ignorance, ineptitude, and corruption.

Incompetence, he wrote, was rewarded, while excellence brought "suspicion, derision, and dismissal." The administration's plans to annex the Dominican Republic were farcical. Its attempts to get rid of congressional opponents were deplorable. Dissident Republicans were upset that Grant had seemingly become indifferent to civil service reforms and had declined to ease radical reconstruction.[5]

Grant was a great general, truly a hero to many, but he was terribly miscast as President. He had no prior experience in government and was apathetic to questions of public policy. An early supporter wondered aloud if Grant had any idea what it actually meant to be President in America's system of government. His appointments to Cabinet posts were often capricious and based solely on personal considerations. Grant took personally any criticisms of his policies and was unduly influenced by a bevy of "parasites."[6]

By January 1872, Bowles was thoroughly fed up. But what was to be done? Three options were open to Bowles and other Republican Party dissidents: stay within the party framework, using their influence to change the party; start a new political organization; or ally themselves with the Democrats. The problem with the first option was that Grant had the nomination sewn up and his cronies were in no mood to change the status quo from which they directly profited. Joining the Democrats would compromise many principles long held. How could they align themselves with a party that was hostile to the rights of black people and that helped cause "the great war?" There was, therefore, only one viable option, a new movement or party.[7]

The Liberal Republican Party movement originated in Missouri, where Governor B. Gratz Brown and Senator Carl Schurz spearheaded the cause. The embryonic group first met in Missouri's capital, Jefferson City, in late January 1872. The insurgents declared the Republican Party organization to be corrupt and a worthless vehicle for reforms. A national meeting in Cincinnati was called for May 1, prior to the regularly scheduled Republican and Democratic conventions.[8]

Bowles strongly backed the incipient movement from the start. The *Republican* was outspoken in its support for the Cincinnati Convention and even more strident in its denunciation of Grant's administration. Bowles considered it his duty "to do everything possible to make [the] convention a great body both in numbers and in character." He declared that he would not be a delegate to the convention or a candidate for office; he was willing to counsel and advise, but not be a "political operator."[9]

Bowles knew that success would not be easy. Several roadblocks stood in the way of reform. The average Republican was still haunted "by the ghost of the Democracy" for one thing. Bowles wrote that although many Republican Party officials agreed with the reformers privately, they were reluctant to jeopardize their positions by supporting the insurgency. Another problem was that the Democratic Party represented to some a decent alternative.[10]

Pessimistic about the movement's chances in January, he grew more optimistic as spring approached. By mid-April, Bowles wrote that the reform movement had grown larger than he had ever anticipated.[11] At the same time, in a ringing editorial, he listed the leading political questions of the day: "Shall the government be administered in the interests of the whole people, or, as in late years, in that of a party, a faction, or a person? Shall the people retain the right of local self-government, . . . or [be] governed more and more from Washington? Shall the memories and rancors of the war be perpetuated by a policy of . . . hate . . . or shall . . . patriotism and national unity . . . be allowed full play under a policy of generous amnesty and reconciliation?"[12]

Bowles arrived early in Cincinnati, the "Queen City of the West." The Ohio River city was filled with delegates. Hotels were so crowded that some slept in lobbies and corridors.[13] Bowles believed that four men had a realistic shot at the nomination—Senator Charles Sumner of Massachusetts, *New York Tribune* editor Horace Greeley, Illinois Senator Lyman Trumbull, and former Ambassador to England Charles Francis Adams of Massachusetts. Bowles praised Greeley and the two senators, who were undoubtedly qualified for the presidency. He lavished special praise, however, on Charles Francis Adams, whom he admired more than any other man in public life. Earlier he had backed Adams for governor and senator, and now he was supporting him for president.[14]

Bowles' adulation for Adams was recalled in a story by his friend Richard Lathers. The over-tired editor was in church one Sunday morning. The minister was preaching a sermon on the Last Judgement and graphically presented the horrors of the Day of Doom, ending with the "vociferous" question: "Who will be able to stand in that great day?" This aroused the semi-conscious Bowles. He rubbed his eyes, arose, and in a most emphatic tone, replied: "Charles Francis Adams! And I nominate him for the position!!!"[15]

As the convention opened, Bowles was surprised at the delegate strength of Illinois' David Davis. A former campaign manager of Abraham Lincoln, Davis was a Supreme Court Justice. Bowles and three compatriots, Murat Halstead of the *Cincinnati Commercial*, Horace White of the *Chicago Tribune*, and Henry Watterson of the *Louisville Courier-Journal*, schemed to torpedo Davis' chances. The four men—later to be known as the "Quadralateral"—attacked Davis in their own newspapers from a different angle. All the pieces were then published together in Halstead's *Commercial*.[16] Their strategy worked, as Davis' candidacy collapsed.

On May 3, Bowles wrote confidently that Adams' nomination was all but certain.[17] The impatient delegates, wanting to get straight to the voting, dispensed with nominating speeches. The first ballot ended with Adams ahead, but without the required majority, Greeley second, Trumbull third, and Missouri Governor Brown last. Brown then withdrew his name and threw his support to Greeley. This move was designed to get back at his in-state political foe, Carl Schurz, a staunch Adams supporter. Ballot followed ballot as Adams failed to make the necessary majority. Gradually, some votes shifted to Greeley, and others followed, creating a bandwagon effect. Aided by the adroit maneuvering of Bowles' friend Whitelaw Reid, an editor at Greeley's *Tribune*, Greeley captured the nomination.[18]

The convention's heart had prevailed over its head. Bowles was certain that no one was more qualified than Adams to be president. His long governmental experience and unimpeachable integrity were well-known. His personality, however, was not one of a politician. He was cold, aloof, and austere, not unlike his famed descendants. His position, that he would accept the nomination but not "peddle with [anyone] for power," displeased delegates who thought him condescending.[19]

Greeley was a familiar figure nationwide. The controversial editor had built the *New York Tribune* into perhaps America's best newspaper. He had been a prominent figure in previous reform movements, and he liked to identify himself with the masses. "Uncle Horace" left an indelible impression on those who saw him. An awkward man, he had a large round face, a bald head, a fringe of white whiskers, drooped eye-glasses, and crumpled clothes with his pockets often stuffed with newspapers. His white hat and squeaky voice did little to detract from his eccentric appearance.[20]

The disappointed members of the quadralateral met right after Greeley's nomination. Watterson, White, and Halstead agreed with Bowles that Greeley had won the nomination fairly, that there was no conspiracy.[21] As to what action to take, only one course was open, they agreed, and that was to back Greeley.[22] Late that evening, Bowles wired confidential instructions to the Republican office that the Greeley-Brown ticket should be supported, but warned his writers not to "gush" over it.[23] He then sat down and wrote his own dispatch to the paper. He praised Greeley's "large and varied ability," and he argued that Greeley represented the best chance for sectional peace, military reform, and the limitations of executive power and patronage. Greeley was the champion of the American workingman. Adams' strength, Bowles believed, would have worked down from the rich and cultured classes. Greeley's strength, he was certain, would develop from the laborer, the poor, and the discontented.[24]

Privately, Bowles was less enthusiastic. He admitted to one friend that he supported Greeley basically because he was the lesser of two evils.[25] Another of Bowles' friends, famed landscape architect Frederick Law Olmstead, was shocked that Bowles was in Greeley's camp. "A thousand years of Grant," Olmstead wrote, "was better than one minute of Greeley."[26] Olmstead called it the darkest day he had ever known when such a man as Samuel Bowles was supporting Horace Greeley. "Bull Run," Olmstead fumed, "was bright to it."[27] Bowles' reply was sympathetic—"your wrath is something refreshing to behold in these days of easy compliance and feeble virtue . . . ."[28]

In early June, Bowles reported from Philadelphia's Academy of Music where the mainstream Republicans were meeting. Contrary to recent rumors, Bowles assured his readers, there was no doubt that incumbent Schuyler Colfax would beat back any challenge for the vice-presidential nomination.[29] Bowles was wrong. Colfax, his close friend and western travelling companion, was dumped.[30] Henry

Wilson, the junior senator from Massachusetts, joined Grant on the ticket.[31] In assessing the delegates, Bowles noted that most were "business men, materialists, men of fact and reality,—not reformers, not leaders in principles . . . ." He admitted, however, that even the second class of the old Republican Party was "of no mean quality of men."[32]

In July, the Democrats met in Baltimore. Surrendering to expediency, they also nominated Greeley and, for good measure, adopted the Liberal Republican Party platform, word for word. Many political observers were astounded. After all, it was Greeley himself who had long blasted the Democrats as "traitors, slave whippers, saloon keepers, horse thieves and idiots." General William Tecumseh Sherman wrote from Paris to his brother, John, Ohio's Republican Senator: "I feel amazed to see the turn things have taken. Grant who never was a Republican is your candidate; and Greeley who never was a Democrat, but quite the reverse, is the Democratic candidate." Greeley getting the Democratic nod did make sense in one important way: he had called for reconciliation, for a clasping of hands across "the bloody chasm."[33] Bowles figured that the desire of the south to be forgiven and have their sins forgotten would also appeal to northerners and enable Greeley to win.[34]

The ensuing campaign proved difficult for Bowles. Many of his friends and associates remained loyal to Grant. Especially upsetting to Bowles was the strong support Congressman and friend Henry L. Dawes gave to Grant. Bowles wished his pragmatic friend "had a little more courage . . . ," but he understood that Dawes' political career might have been imperiled by not backing Grant.[35] He was even more upset and saddened, however, at the tone and vehemence of Dawes' attack on Greeley and his supporters.[36] Bowles was hurt when, after "gross personal attacks" were written on his character, Dawes failed to come to his defense. The *Republican*, Bowles wrote Dawes, has always "promptly, explicitly, and repeatedly" defended your character.[37]

The campaign was a dirty one. Issues were ignored as both sides resorted to name-calling and character assassination. Greeley was denounced as an atheist, a Communist, a free-love advocate, a vegetarian, a "brown-bread eater," and worse. His co-signing of Jefferson Davis' bail bond struck a raw nerve in many Union veterans and others who lost relatives in the war. Grant, on the other hand, was derided as an ignoramus, a drunkard, and a crook.[38] The campaign dragged on through the long, hot summer and into the fall. Greeley stumped the nation tirelessly while Grant, more traditionally had others campaign on his behalf.

Greeley was thoroughly whipped; he carried only six border and southern states. His own home state of New York rejected his candidacy by more than fifty thousand votes. Bowles was not surprised at the outcome. Greeley never recovered from his stinging defeat. His beloved *Tribune* crippled, he sank into "acute, nervous prostration" and died a brokenhearted man.[39]

While Greeley's *Tribune* suffered during the campaign, Bowles' *Republican* felt the iron hand of the Grant administration as well. The *Weekly Republican's* circulation dropped by about a thousand copies in the election year, as western Massachusetts postmasters—loyal to Grant as their jobs depended on his re-election—refused to deliver Bowles' paper throughout much of the region. Bowles blasted such action as "vindictive and mean," as a blatant attempt to quash "independent journalism."[40] Normal deliveries resumed, however, shortly after Grant's victory.

Eighteen seventy-two was an important year for the embattled editor for reasons other than political. In the midst of the electoral tumult, Bowles decided to dissolve the partnership of Samuel Bowles and Company. Through early 1872, ownership of Samuel Bowles and Company was vested in a few people. Bowles owned the leading interest while most of the remainder was divided among Clark Bryan, J. F. Tapley, and Bowles' younger brother, Benjamin. The *Republican* was under Samuel's editorial control, Benjamin was in charge of bookkeeping, Bryan ran the general printing business, and Tapley took care of the binding. From all outward appearances, the business functioned smoothly. At some point, however, in the winter of 1872, Bowles decided to dissolve the partnership and completely separate the newspaper from the printing and binding departments. He had two major reasons. First and foremost was Bowles' desire, with controlling interest in the *Republican*, to pass it on to his family—especially to his son Samuel—upon his death. Bowles also wanted to free himself from the other departments that had experienced enormous growth in recent years. He also felt his health would improve by eliminating any role in non-editorial matters.

Once his mind was made up, Bowles was a determined man. He sought out Bryan one Sunday morning after church. As they strolled through the lovely Armory grounds, Bowles turned to his partner and friend of twenty years and said brusquely that there had to be a division of the concern into two separate firms. Bryan replied that such a move was against everyone's interest. Bowles responded, "I'm tired of making money for other people." Bryan was crushed, and he promptly agreed to Bowles' demand. Tapley and Ben Bowles were also distraught when they received the news. There was, however, little they could do but go along. Shortly afterwards, Bowles proposed that he retain a small interest in Bryan's and Tapley's firm and that Bryan likewise retain a small interest in the *Republican*. Perhaps for the first time in his life, Bryan stood firm; he told Bowles that he would only agree to a one-hundred percent separation. Several weeks later, the dissolution was legalized.[41]

Shortly after the break-up came a new development that shocked Bowles. Since the death of the *Springfield Argus*, a Democratic Party organ, in the late 1850s, the *Republican* had no daily competition until the founding of the *Springfield Evening Union* in 1864. For eight years, the *Union* provided negligible competition.[42] That soon changed, however, as Bryan and Tapley purchased the Union printing company and its most important product, the *Springfield Evening Union*. The new competition was now owned by Clark W. Bryan and Company. Bowles commented on the changes in Springfield's newspaper arena, insisting that the recent changes were "not the result of personal or public differences."[43]

The *Union*, a Grant supporter from the outset, gained the political sympathy of much of the *Republican's* old constituency. Numerous people "injured" by the *Republican* over the years now purchased the opposition newspaper. Competition from the *Union* forced Bowles to lower advertising rates in the *Republican*. Conditions worsened for Bowles when a wholesale exodus of *Republican* staffers accepted Bryan's offer to work for the *Union*. The harshest blow was the resignation of managing editor William Pomeroy—Bowles' right-hand man—to take a similar position under Bryan.[44]

As a sign of good-will, Bowles threw a dinner party for the departing Pomeroy and invited Bryan by letter, urging his attendance as a sign of unbroken friendship. Bryan came to the party. The two men spoke and were cordial, but the bond of friendship had been irrevocably torn. The general consensus in the community was that Bryan had been wronged. Bryan, somewhat intimidated by Bowles in person, got back at his former boss through the pages of the *Union*. Bowles refused to reply. It was, indeed, for Samuel Bowles "a long dreary summer."[45]

Ironically, the harried editor who was looking to ease his burden found that it dramatically increased. Bowles vowed to put out an even better newspaper, and he added hours to an already long work day. Bowles was forced to do the work of three or four men as he began to train new people for the positions created by the recent resignations. He had planned a vacation in Europe or Colorado. Instead, he stayed in Springfield.[46] On New Year's Day, 1873, Bowles looked back at one of the most difficult years in his life and declared 1872 "devoid of history."[47]

NOTES

1. *S.R.*, January 2, 1872, p. 2, col. I.

2. Ibid., January 9, 1872, p. 2, col. I.

3. Ibid., January 16, 1872, p. 2, col. I.

4. Ibid., January 29, 1872, p. 2, col. II. Bowles was so proud of his new operation that he invited the public in on Wednesday and Thursday afternoons to watch the weekly *Republican* being printed.

5. William Gillet, "Election of 1872," in *History of American Presidential Elections,* edited by Arthur Schlesinger, Jr. (New York: Chelsea House Publishers in Association with McGraw-Hill, 1971), II:1306.

6. Merriam, II:111-114. For the life of Grant, see William McFeely, *Grant: A Biography* (New York: W. W. Norton, 1981).

7. Ibid., pp. 167-177.

8. Gillet, p. 1306.

9. Bowles to Edward Atkinson, March 9, 1872, in Edward Atkinson Papers, Massachusetts Historical Society, Boston, and Bowles to B. Gratz Brown, April 15, 1872, Bowles Papers. Bowles was a political operator of the first order. He sincerely believed that exclusion from party office or technical affiliation made him "independent" and above the dirty-doings of political give-and-take.

10. Bowles to Carl Schurz, March 22, 1872, in Carl Schurz, *Speeches, Correspondence, Political Papers*, (New York: Putnam and Sons, 1913), II:353, Bowles to Sumner, March 30, 1872, Bowles Papers, and *S.R.*, March 6, 1872, p. 5, col. VI.

11. Bowles to Dawes, April 15, 1872, Dawes Papers and W. H. Huntington to John Bigelow, April 11, 1872, in John Bigelow, *Retrospections on an Active Life* (Garden City: Doubleday, 1913), V:20.

12. Merriam, II:179.

13. Gillet, p. 1309.

14. Hooker, p. 114.

15. Alvan F. Sanborn, editor, *Reminiscences of Richard Lather* (Grafton Press, 1908), p. 332.

16. Gillet, p. 1309.

17. *S.R.*, May 3, 1872, p. 4, col. V.

18. Merriam, II:186-187. One local merchant responded to Greeley's nomination with the advertisement: "Greeley is nominated but Grant still reigns at 395 Main." Springfield's Grant sold Parlor Spittoons. See *S.R.*, May 4, 1872, p. 8, col. II.

19. Merriam, II:181.

20. Ibid.

21. Matthew Downer, "Horace Greeley and the Politicians: The Liberal Republican Convention in 1872," *Journal of American History* (March 1967), p. 728.

22. Merriam, II:187.

23. Hooker, p. 115.

24. Merriam, II:188.

25. Bowles to Dawes, May 28, 1872, Dawes Papers.

26. Frederick Law Olmstead to Bowles, May 7, 1872, Olmstead Papers, Library of Congress.

27. Ibid., May 13, 1872.

28. Bowles to Olmstead, May 15, 1872. Bowles and Olmstead became fast friends. Their values were similar, they suffered from insomnia and dyspepsia, and both were workaholics. See Laura Wood Roper, *F.L.O.: A Biography of Frederick Law Olmstead* (Baltimore: Johns Hopkins University Press, 1973), p. 287. Bowles tried to get Olmstead to move to Springfield and become a consulting landscape architect. See Bowles to Olmstead, June 14, 1871, Olmstead Papers, Library of Congress.

29. *S.R.*, June 3, 1872, p. 4, col. IV.

30. Bowles lost an important pipeline for Washington news and gossip. See for example, Colfax to Bowles, January 20, 1869, Colfax Papers, Indiana State Library, Indianapolis.

31. Bowles, of course, knew Wilson as he did every major political leader in Massachusetts. Their relationship blew hot and cold over the years depending on the particular issue and election involved.

32. Merriam, II:190.

33. Bailey, p. 457.

34. Merriam, II:211-212.

35. Bowles to Dawes, July 16, 1872, Dawes Papers.

36. Bowles to Dawes, August 22, 1872, ibid.

37. Bowles to Dawes, August 22, 1872, ibid.

38. Bailey, p. 457.

39. Merriam, II:200.

40. Bowles to Dawes, February 10, 1873, Dawes Papers. Never before had Bowles and the *Republican* been so at odds politically with its citizenry. Bowles remarked that up until 1872, the paper was "the political bible" of western Massachusetts. See Griffin, p. 132.

41. Merriam, II:201-204. Bowles had spent much time in non-editorial business. See, for example, his letters to Newton Bateman, October 21 and November 9, 1871, and January 4, 1872, in the Illinois State Library, Springfield, Illinois.

42. Hooker, p. 119.

43. *S.R.*, May 31, 1872, p. 2, col. III.

44. Merriam, II:205.

45. Ibid., pp. 206-208.

46. Hooker, p. 120.

47. Elizabeth Ryan, "Samuel Bowles: Pioneer in Independent Journalism," Mount Holyoke College Honors Paper, 1936, p. 58.

CHAPTER VIII

BACK INTO THE POLITICAL FRAY

Bowles looked forward to the new year. After all, he must have thought, how could things be worse than a reform movement overwhelmingly rejected by the voters and a business dissolution gone awry? Bowles kept busy training his young, new staff. Two former newspapermen, Wilmot Warren and Charles G. Whiting, returned to the *Republican* at his request. He hired young Solomon B. Griffin, a scholarly, eager pupil who carried out Bowles' instructions to the letter. Bowles' most important new staffer, however, was his twenty-one year old son Samuel. Bowles wanted his son versed in all facets of the newspaper, so he trained him as a reporter and editor, as well as in financial and technical matters.[1]

Politically, Bowles' interest focused on the United States Senate seat vacated by the Vice-President-elect, Henry Wilson. Bowles supported his close friend, Congressman Henry L. Dawes. Former Massachusetts Governor George Boutwell opposed Dawes, and the state legislature chose Boutwell. Shortly afterwards another vacancy was created by the death of Senator Charles Sumner. Dawes ran again, this time opposed by Judge Ebenezer Rockwood Hoar of Concord. Fierce infighting broke out in the legislature this time. Bowles was upset that Dawes did not repudiate the support of Benjamin Butler, an old Bowles foe. From all outward appearances, it seemed as if Dawes was actually bargaining for support, an unconscionable sin in Bowles' mind. Several weeks of balloting failed to produce a winner, but finally the deadlock ended when the legislature chose Governor Washburn for the Senate seat.[2]

Bowles believed that politics and politicians should be "pure." Bargaining or deals were repugnant to the reformist editor. Earlier, when Dawes and James G. Blaine opposed each other for Speaker of the House, Bowles and Blaine exchanged a series of letters that were made public. The duel was closely followed in political and journalistic circles. Blaine had openly solicited votes for himself among House members, and that upset Bowles. The question involved, he wrote Blaine, was "one of taste, and modes of political advancement. We, that is the *Republican*, hold somewhat fastidious notions on the subject . . . . I have no sympathy with the popular means of preferment in which you seem to have very liberally indulged." Bowles took pains to add that he personally liked Blaine very much.[3]

An angered Blaine replied the next day. He asked Bowles to specify exactly what he had done to offend his "fastidious notions." He declared that Bowles was operating with assumptions, not facts, and that he might be better off applying "some fastidious notions to the science of journalism." Blaine claimed that he had not done anything during the contest "that was in any way offensive to Mr. Dawes—of that I have Mr. Dawes' personal assurance." Blaine closed by noting that although the letter was marked "personal," he would not be surprised to see it published in the *Republican*.[4]

Two weeks passed before Bowles read Blaine's letter, as he had been ill and had an out-of-town commitment. When he finally read it, he was sorry he had read it at all. The overly-sensitive Bowles called it "inexcusably ill-tempered and insulting" and he refused to reply to Blaine's specific charges.[5] Blaine, therefore, sent Bowles another letter demanding that Bowles back up his charge that he, Blaine, had resorted to "personal beggary" and "corrupt practices" to advance his election as Speaker.[6] Bowles replied that he knew that Blaine had personally solicited votes and personally superintended the election. Both these acts, Bowles insisted, were unethical, improper, "a scandal to the country and a scandal to Congress."[7] Within twenty-four hours, Blaine responded: "I can say with absolute truth that I never *solicited* a vote . . . ."[8] Several days later, Bowles agreed to end—for the time being—the entire matter.[9] Dawes praised Bowles for his conduct in the Blaine affair. Dawes was dumbfounded by Blaine's account of the contest for House Speaker. "If Blaine is telling the truth," he wrote to Bowles, "then half the house must be liars."[10]

Meanwhile, in 1873, the nation found itself in a severe economic depression. Overenthusiastic promoters had laid more railroad track, sunk more mines, built more factories, and plowed more wheat fields than the existing markets could absorb. Bankers, in turn, had made too many unwise loans to budding entrepreneurs. When profits failed to materialize, the loans went unpaid, and the nation's economy suffered. "Boom times became gloom times" as fifteen thousand businesses went under and widespread unemployment developed. The Panic of 1873 marked the beginning of the worst economic depression the nation had experienced to that time.[11]

Springfield had prospered in the post-bellum period. In eight short years since war's end, the central business district had expanded by a remarkable sixty percent.[12] Samuel Bowles and the *Republican* aided the city's growth by its boosterism. The financial woes of the nation, however, soon caught up to the "City of Homes."[13] In those troubled times, the cry for new leadership echoed across the city. The people of Springfield turned to Sam Bowles, asking him to be their mayor. Bowles received two petitions, both with the same message: "The undersigned legal voters of Springfield . . . respectfully request your acceptance of a citizen's nomination for Mayor . . . ." The first petition was signed by a handful of Springfield's elite. The other was signed by hundreds of "ordinary" residents.[14]

The impetus behind the Bowles trial balloon came from a most surprising source, the rival *Springfield Union*. "Unexpected and astonishing," Bowles wrote, was "the complimentary invitation to be mayor that has come out of the *Union's* advocacy." Bowles found the offer embarrassing, but also gratifying. Indeed, he termed the offer "the highest and most agreeable compliment" of his life. Bowles was also touched by the "high praise" that Bryan's *Union* had bestowed upon him.[15]

Bowles flirted with the idea of running, but ultimately refused. In a public letter he wrote that he would rather be Mayor of Springfield than hold any other political office. He was proud of Springfield, and relished the opportunity to come closer to "its people and its institutions." But, Bowles added, he felt obliged to decline. He did not have the time or the strength to run Springfield. Bowles believed he could best help Springfield "by undivided service in his profession." He closed by noting once more that asking him to be mayor transcended all other compliments and honors of his life.[16]

That year's mayoral contest spawned an unexpected consequence, another libel suit against Samuel Bowles and the *Springfield Republican*. The campaign's major issue centered on railroad expansion.

The owner of the Athol and Enfield, a new Massachusetts railroad that linked central Vermont with the Connecticut shoreline, requested local funds for an extension of its tracks to Springfield. Springfield's Willis Phelps owned the Athol and Enfield. The sixty-five year old railroad tycoon had lived in Springfield since his teens. A pillar of the Methodist Church and active in a variety of civic affairs, Phelps was also one of Springfield's wealthiest men. Phelps was a self-made man, unschooled, shrewd, manipulative, and a man of questionable ethics. His tactlessness, bluntness, and overbearing personality had made him more than a few enemies. Phelps' new plan threatened the interests of two other local railroad magnates, Daniel Harris and Chester Chapin, both close friends of Samuel Bowles. Detractors pointed to a study of the Massachusetts Railroad Commission that reported that existing stretches of the Athol could not "be said to be either well or thoroughly built, nor could it sustain any considerable traffic and continue safe." Other Phelps' critics cited the unusually large number of windfalls made by Phelps' allies, and the allegedly disreputable methods Phelps had used to get a charter from the legislature.[17]

Phelps had his supporters in town, however, who argued that Phelps had a proven record in delivering railroads, while others had made only promises. Armory Hill interests supported Phelps because the proposed road would link that area to other outlying parts of Springfield. The city council vigorously debated Phelps' request for $150,000, and rejected it. That precipitated a fierce political debate in the summer and fall of 1873 that culminated in James Thompson's mayoral nomination being thwarted by an unruly caucus. Phelps, very likely the power-broker behind the scenes, was quoted as saying, "You can't have him. You can't have anyone who is opposed to the road."[18]

Bowles steamed as Phelps apparently got his way. The *Republican* lashed out at him with a vitriolic attack. "TWEEDISM IN SPRINGFIELD" blazed the headline, followed by a scorching text that said in part: "Mr. Willis Phelps is the Boss Tweed of Springfield. He openly bids for a city 'job;' he goes to the Legislature and lobbies through a bill . . . with the help of votes he buys, he openly carries an election."[19] Several days later the *Republican* added, "Mr. Phelps proved himself in the Athol transaction a public robber and a public corrupter, and he is now repeating the exhibition in the most audacious and flagrant manner."[20]

106

Willis Phelps

Phelps fought back; he brought suit against the *Republican* for $200,000 damages. A writ of attachment to secure the money was issued against the *Republican*, and an interruption of its publication loomed large. But Bowles, acting speedily, got the signatures of many well-to-do area residents guaranteeing the payment of damages, if awarded.[21]

Bowles informed his readers, under the headline: "A Welcome Libel Suit." The issue is clear, he wrote, "Was the *Republican* justified in exposing the character of the transactions and denouncing the man responsible for them in the decided and harsh language that it used?" Bowles added that the *Republican* was shocked by rumors that the whole affair stemmed from Phelps not signing the letter for Bowles' mayoral petition. "Mr. Bowles never before knew that Mr. Phelps even had a chance to refuse to sign the letter in question and never cared. There were enough names on that letter to insure Mr. Bowles' election [anyway] . . . ."[22]

Bowles began a search for the best lawyer available, and he also began research in preparation for his own defense. During the winter of 1874, he was totally preoccupied with the case. But when the suit was called for trial in April, both sides agreed to a postponement. The trial would not begin until a full year later.[23]

Meanwhile, the exhausted Bowles needed a rest. An opportunity to get away presented itself, and he took advantage of it. One day in mid-summer, 1874, he met railroad mogul Chester Chapin getting ready to sail from Boston the next day for a European holiday. "Come with me, as my companion and guest," said Chapin. Bowles hesitated, although not for long, and accepted the generous offer. The two men stayed in London and Paris, and were joined, at one point, by Bowles' recently-married daughter and son-in-law, who were abroad on their honeymoon. Bowles saw many friends like George Smally of the *New York Tribune* and Murat Halstead of the *Cincinnati Commercial*.[24] Bowles had a grand time. He and his friends swapped stories, exchanged gossip, and, on occasion, amused themselves to such an extent that "hardly a dry eye was left in the House."[25] Bowles planned to relax and he avoided any sightseeing. He slept ten hours a night, took leisurely strolls, and played a great deal of cards and backgammon. His vacation, Bowles wrote approvingly, was "one prolonged spree of a mild moral type, rather elevating and altogether dissipating."[26] Chapin proved to be an agreeable travelling companion, and Bowles characterized him as "very amiable and courteous and submissive," although, Bowles admitted, he wished Chapin was "a trifle more inspiring."[27]

Bowles returned home in October and found himself once again in the thick of local politics. Henry L. Dawes had declined to run for re-election to the western Massachusetts congressional seat he had filled for nearly two decades. Dawes had his eyes on the Senate. Bowles thought that Dawes had made a mistake, but added that "the people of no congressional district in the Union have been more ably, faithfully, and satisfactorily represented than his western Massachusetts constituency."[28] The question was who would replace the popular Dawes?[29] The Democrats nominated Bowles' vacation companion, millionaire Chester Chapin. The Republican Party selected former Springfield mayor and bank president Henry Alexander. Nine times out of ten Bowles and his paper backed Republican Party candidates, but not this time. On principle, Bowles could not support Alexander—his own brother-in-law.

Alexander's candidacy represented to Bowles the worst features of the political process. Bowles strongly objected to the procedure—a stacked caucus at a district convention—that won Alexander the nomination. Alexander's bid symbolized to Bowles the ascendency of the seamier side in public life. "It is the misfortune of this candidate—to put the fact in the most charitable way," Bowles wrote, "that it is backed by men, interests, ambitions, combinations, and methods which ought never to be allowed to make a Massachusetts congressman."[30] Bowles returned from the district convention deeply depressed. He confided to an old friend that the day had "parted hands that will be joined over a coffin." Another friend suggested that he should keep the *Republican* out of the impending battle and "go a fishing." Bowles answered simply, "The *Republican* has no brother-in-law."[31]

At the campaign's outset, Bowles wrote Alexander a frank letter urging him to reconsider his congressional quest. "I should record it as my solemn judgement," Bowles noted ruefully, "that your running for Congress will be the great mistake, possibly the great crime of your life." He warned Alexander that his health could not bear the strain of running for office; that if he should win, "The experiences and responsibilities . . . would almost surely break you down and carry you to your grave!" On the other hand, "the mortifi-

Chester Chapin

cation and disgrace of defeat," might prove equally fatal. He added that although he opposed him "with great regret and sorrow," he would be unsparingly critical in the pages of his newspaper. He closed by asking Alexander to forgive him for what he had to do publicly as a journalist.[32]

Bowles held nothing back. In a rare move, he reprinted an editorial from the rival *Springfield Union*, which found Alexander "objectionable to a great many Republicans of the better class," and complained about the method of his nomination. The *Union* found it "impossible to get up any enthusiasm for him," and maintained that if he were elected he would "not make a member of Congress the district could be proud of."[33] That same day Bowles editorialized about Alexander. As he had written privately, he now publicly stated that Alexander was making the mistake of his life. Bowles wrote that Alexander's nomination brought "grief to everyone who has a genuine liking for the man." Alexander, Bowles stated positively, had "been cruelly hoodwinked and betrayed in cold blood" by men whose only interest in him was purely selfish and calculating. Behind him, Bowles continued, were "the worst men, the worst practices, and the worst tendencies" in local politics. Bowles declared that his sister's husband fronted for the "traders, vote mongers, and rings."[34]

Bowles said little about the rich and unrefined Chapin. Chapin, much to Bowles' liking, had been an independent Democrat. Bowles informed his readers, as proof, that in 1862, when the Democrats wanted Chapin to oppose Dawes, he had refused, saying that "Dawes is a good enough Congressman for me."[35]

As the New England foliage glistened that autumn, Bowles continued his attack. He reiterated his belief that Alexander's candidacy stood for all that was "corrupt and mischievous, in fact or in tendency, in modern American politics." He added that the forthcoming election challenged "every honest, thoughtful, patriotic citizen, who has professed to see danger to the country in the growing corruption of its politics."[36]

As the bitter campaign drew to a close, Bowles stopped attacking Alexander for what he symbolized, and went at him personally. Bowles claimed that Alexander himself was "the king of caucus management and ring rule" in Springfield politics, and he also lashed out at "Boss" Tinker, Alexander's mentor in Berkshire County.[37]

Chapin won the election.[38] Bowles still thought Chapin foolish in wanting a congressional seat, but he realized "that the seduction was too great." The seventy-six year old Chapin had satisfied a life-long ambition, Bowles figured, "the recognition and endorsement of his fellow men."[39] Bowles' man won, but at a price—the loss of a dear sister. Amelia Alexander's contempt spilled out in a letter to her brother, with whom she refused to speak face to face: "the lies and slanders . . . which you knew to be such that have been published in the *Republican* . . . have filled our hearts with bitterness and hatred towards you which I fear time cannot efface . . . you have broken our family relations."[40]

Several months later, Henry Alexander wrote to Bowles, enclosing a tax bill which he had previously paid for Bowles. He wanted Bowles to know that his health was poor. More importantly, he recommended divestiture of their joint property held in Springfield. Closing, he wrote, "Yours not mistakingly, though cruelly abused."[41]

NOTES

1. Merriam, II:308. Merriam wrote that the *Republican* "under its new circumstances" was a better newspaper than it had ever been. He contended that anybody who goes through the old newspaper will see it plainly. As one who did just that, this author did not see any marked difference.

2. Ibid., pp. 264-266. Bowles and Dawes were close friends most of their adult lives. They disagreed politically only in one major instance: Dawes' support of Grant in 1872. When Dawes sent congratulations to the Bowles on their twenty-fifth wedding anniversary (Dawes to Bowles, September 6, 1873, Dawes Papers), Bowles was deeply touched. He replied, " . . . we didn't dream that you were aware of the anniversary. No other of our friends were, and your letter therefore stands out alone . . . ." See Bowles to Dawes, September 13, 1873, Dawes Papers.

3. Bowles to James G. Blaine, March 23, 1869, Bowles Papers. No one but Bowles believed a distinction existed between his own thoughts and the *Republican*. Bowles pummeled political figures like Blaine and Butler, at the same time contending that he liked them personally. He wrote that there was no one more personable and better to meet "when business is over" than Ben Butler. But when Butler gets into politics "and makes of statesmanship a police court and corner grocery business, then we are obliged to painfully differ and deal out to him 'the blows of a friend.'" See Ryan, p. 36.

4. Blaine to Bowles, March 24, 1869, Bowles Papers.

5. Bowles to Blaine, April 6, 1869.

6. Blaine to Bowles, April 7, 1869.

7. Bowles to Blaine, April 9, 1869.

8. Blaine to Bowles, April 10, 1869.

9. Bowles to Blaine, April 13, 1869.

10. Dawes to Bowles, April 18, 1869, Dawes Papers.

11. Bailey, p. 458, and Potter, p. 213.

12. Frisch, p. 141.

13. The Panic hurt the *Republican* also "right in the heart of the advertising season." Bowles was forced to "enforce economy along the whole line." See Merriam, II:335.

14. Both petitions dated November 14, 1873 are in the Bowles Papers.

15. Merriam, II:337. Bryan's motives may have been less than pure. If Bowles had become mayor, the *Republican* would have been deprived of one of America's best newspaper editors. It is doubtful that the *Republican* could have kept up its superior quality.

16. There were other reasons, not publicly admitted, why Bowles chose not to run. First of all, as he admitted to his associate Frank B. Sanborn, he could not afford it. See Merriam, II:335. Bowles had seven children and a beautiful home to support. Perhaps, more importantly, he feared losing; his election was no sure thing. "Special Correspondent 'VALE'" wrote an interesting analysis in the *Chicago Times* (May 29, 1873, copy in Bowles Papers): "The *Republican* has managed to step upon a great many people's corns. There is a very large number of persons who cherish personal grievances . . . against its editor, and who would like nothing better than a chance to express their opinion of him through the unostentatious medium of the ballot box . . . another class . . . abhors the

iconoclastic spirit of the *Republican* . . . another class, not so large but more virulent, . . . who through one circumstance or another have been thrown in personal contact with Bowles . . . not infrequently asking redress or apology for some gross wrong done them through a false or distorted account of this or that affair (in the *Republican*)." Vale added that many employees who suffered from Bowles' arbitrary manner may have voted against him. Vale makes some good points, but conveniently leaves out the fact that many people loved and strongly admired the man. Springfield residents were proud of Bowles' fame and/or notoriety as well as the *Republican's* glowing national reputation.

17. Frisch, p. 185.

18. Ibid., p. 187.

19. *S.R.*, November 29, 1873, p. 4. col. II.

20. Frisch, p. 187. In the election, a majority of voters did not share Bowles' concern as they voted in a city council favorable to Phelps' interests.

21. Merriam, II:312.

22. *S.R.*, December 3, 1873, p. 4, col. II.

23. Merriam, II:313. Bowles was afraid that the case would never get to trial. See Bowles to Whitelaw Reid, December 3, 1873 in Reid Papers. He also suffered severe headaches at the time and went to New York City for relief. The doctor punched his head and froze it. See Bowles to Reid, December 9, 1873, Reid Papers.

24. Marietta Hutchinson to Samuel Bowles, July 5, 1874 in Bowles Papers, and Merriam, II:313.

25. Bigelow, V:167.

26. Merriam, II:341. His only health setback was caused by a difficult boat ride across "the horrors of the channel" that produced headaches for a while.

27. Ibid., p. 340.

28. Ibid., p. 267.

29. Bowles probably gave some thought to running himself. Bowles printed an article from *Chicago Times* correspondent "Gideon," that urged him not to accept any offer for Congress. Gideon wrote that "Mr. Bowles' success in journalism has been so eminent, so noble and so valuable that all who love a really grand newspaper dread lest he may be seduced into the easier paths of congressional life." See *S.R.*, July 24, 1874, p. 3, col. I.

30. *S.R.*, October 17, 1874, p. 4, col. I.

31. Merriam, II:315.

32. Bowles to Alexander, October 19, 1874, Bowles Papers. Bowles wrote Dawes that same day declaring that opposing Alexander was perhaps the most disagreeable experience of his life. See Bowles to Dawes, October 19, 1874, Dawes Papers.

33. *S.R.*, October 21, 1874, p. 5, col. I.

34. Ibid., p. 4, col. I.

35. Ibid., October 15, 1874, p. 4, col. I. Of course, as most knew, the chances of a Democrat winning election to Congress in the North during the Civil War were mighty slim. Chapin was not stupid.

36. *S.R.*, October 22, 1874, p. 4, col. II.

37. Ibid., November 2, 1874, p. 4, col. III. Bowles despised "Boss" Edward R. Tinker, collector of the Internal Revenue in western Massachusetts. Much to Bowles' chagrin, Tinker was Dawes' chief political lieutenant. See Steven J. Arcanti, "To Secure the Party: Henry L. Dawes and the Politics of Reconstruction," *Historical Journal of Western Massachusetts* (Spring 1977), p. 39. Bowles wrote Dawes: "If you could export Tinker to the Cannibal Islands for six months or get him to retire from his office and into private life, it would be a very great gain . . . some of your best friends say they are repulsed by him." See Bowles to Dawes, October 16, 1874, Dawes Papers.

38. Bowles accepted an all-expanse paid vacation to Europe from Chapin and simultaneously—presumably on ethical or conflict-of-interest grounds—declined free railraod passes for his staff and himself! See Griffin, p. 46. Chapin was so fabulously wealthy he gave each of his children $50,000 as a Christmas present. See *S.R.*, December 27, 1871, p. 8, col. I. For more on Chapin, see Stephen Salsbury, *The State, The Investor, and The Railroad: The Boston & Albany, 1825-1867* (Cambridge: Harvard University Press, 1967), pp. 274-295, passim.

39. Bowles to Murat Halstead, November 9, 1874, in Halstead Papers, Cincinnati Historical Society. In that same year, Bowles admitted that he owed ten times as much to Alexander as he ever did or could to Chapin. He also confessed that Alexander had always been "a very good fellow" to him.

40. Amelia Alexander to Samuel Bowles, November 4, 1874. Bowles Papers.

41. Henry Alexander to Samuel Bowles, April 13, 1875, Bowles Papers.

CHAPTER IX

INDEPENDENT JOURNALISM ON TRIAL

The Chapin-Alexander fray drained Bowles. To anyone within earshot, he would explain that the *Republican* had no other choice but to go after Alexander with all its might. Bowles found solace corresponding with his daughter Sallie, who lived in Germany. He suggested that she write a few letters from Berlin to the *Republican*. Readers, he assured her, would love to know about Berlin's growth, the American colony there, the university, and Bismarck. You are a Bowles, he reminded her gently, with the "newspaper gift, you know . . . ."[1] In early 1875, he wrote a note of congratulations. Sallie had given birth to her first child, making Bowles a grandfather for the first time. It is a considerable thing to be a grandfather, he rejoiced, "when the posterity is of such a character!—but it is 'an almighty big thing' to be a mother!" Bowles lamented the fact that he could not see Sallie and the baby, explaining that almost all his time was spent on the trial preparations.[2]

Finally, after more than a year's delay, the Phelps libel trial was about to begin in Springfield, with Judge William C. Endicott of Salem presiding. Bowles again reported his view of the role of the press in society: "It shall be the conservator of public morals, the guardian of the public treasury and the watch and ward of the general interest . . . ."[3] A week later, on April 23, 1875, Bowles reported that both parties to the suit were in active preparation. He added that there had not been a similar case in Massachusetts in an entire generation.[4]

The trial began on April 26. Under a new law enacted the previous year, by mutual consent both parties in a civil suit could waive a jury trial and leave the verdict entirely up to the judge. Initially, Phelps wanted a jury trial, which was fine with Bowles. Phelps, however, then changed his mind; Bowles had no problem with that either.[5] Judge B. F. Thomas of Boston, M. B. Whitney of Westfield, and Springfield's Henry Morris and A. M. Copeland represented Phelps. Heading the defense team was famed Boston author and attorney Richard Henry Dana, Jr. Aiding Dana were local lawyers E. B. Maynard and N. A. Leonard, along with Bowles' long-time friend Charles Allen of Greenfield. Bowles also spent untold hours in preparation. Indeed, Bowles staked out the main lines of his defense with little help from his attorneys.[6]

Bowles based his defense not only on the general principle of freedom of the press, but also on the truth of the charges made in the *Republican*. This strategy made for colorful testimony as he vigorously sought to prove that Phelps had undermined the legitimate democratic processes at every step. Bowles charged that a packed caucus had sent Phelps' son John to the Massachusetts legislature in 1872 specifically to lobby for the Athol bill that resulted in a referendum question being placed on the Springfield ballot. The voters then approved a subsidy for Phelps' railroad. Bowles then charged that another stacked caucus sent Phelps' other son Henry to the legislature to lobby for another bill for the Longmeadow Road. When this plan failed, Bowles contended that Phelps dumped Colonel Thompson and rigged the 1873 mayoral election.[7] In addition, the defense argued that since C. C. Merritt, the able representative from Phelps' district, opposed building the Springfield and Longmeadow Railroad at city expense, he had to go. Who better than Phelps' own son could best represent the Phelps family business interests? The Phelps then schemed to get rid of Merritt, but they could never succeed by any fair means. Bowles' lawyers argued that the caucus held before the election was known as the single most corrupt caucus ever held in Springfield. Men came from all quarters of the city, from Wards One and Three, men who could vote and men who could not. They came singly and in squads and they jammed the room. Their votes were stuffed into the ballot-box in handfuls. Phelps thus secured the nomination, and his election ensued.[8]

The defense then called a number of colorful characters to testify. An Armory employee named Lyons swore that Phelps asked him to help in the election. Lyons agreed only if Phelps' brother would not run against S. W. Porter for Water Commissioner. Phelps' brother subsequently withdrew his nomination, and Lyons worked for Phelps. Lyons testified that after the election, Phelps paid him $15 to $20 for his services and $25 to $30 for Keating, a Ward Seven saloonkeeper whom Lyons had hired. Lyons added that he saw underage boys voting at the caucus along with fifty to seventy-five foreigners who were not eligible to vote.

Representative Merritt then took the stand and his testimony supported what Lyons had reported. He said that it was more a mob scene than a caucus. He swore that he saw men who didn't live in the district taking an active role in the caucus. He agreed that many French-Canadian workmen from Phelps' railroad had voted illegally.[9] Charles H. Dow, a Providence, Rhode Island, newspaperman and a former reporter for the *Republican*, testified that he had been told that one man had put nineteen ballots in the box. Then a barber testified that he was promised that if he would vote for Phelps, he would receive six months of work.[10]

On the stand himself, Bowles was conciliatory. He informed the court that with Willis Phelps he was once an associate director of the old Longmeadow Railroad Company. Bowles claimed that "he had only kindly feelings" toward Phelps "for twenty-five or thirty years and these feelings have not changed to this day."[11] Bowles then stunned the court by saying that Wilmot L. Warren, of the *Republican* editorial staff, wrote the article "Tweedism in Springfield." Bowles quickly added that he completely supported Warren. Warren then testified that he wrote the article with no personal malice intended. As a matter of fact, he added, he had never seen Phelps.[12]

On May 5, 1875, after nine days of testimony, Judge Endicott handed down his decision as "the little buzz of conversation and speculation was succeeded by a solemn quiet which grew in intensity and impressiveness as his honor proceeded."[13] For the most part, Endicott sided with the *Republican*. He declared that the evidence was conclusive that there were grave improprieties on Phelps' part. He agreed with Bowles that Phelps' influence upon the legislature was unbecoming and dangerous. The judge also declared that although no direct bribery had been proven in the city election, it was obvious that money was freely used and that the influence exerted was essentially corrupt. By and large, Endicott concluded, the *Republican's* charges were supportable except in one instance. The judge cited a passage that said of Phelps: "Having spoiled the city of $200,000, he is now using that money and the power that its expenditure gave him, to despoil her of another sum nearly as large." This charge, the court ruled, had not been proven. As a result, Judge Endicott assessed damages of one hundred dollars against the *Republican*.[14]

When Bowles heard the verdict, he exploded. Despite the fact that the general consensus had the *Republican* a winner, Bowles was furious that the paper had to pay even a nominal amount in damages. He exclaimed: "Damn one hundred dollars; damn a cent!" Both parties later filed exceptions and declared their intentions to carry the case before a full bench of the court. But the appeal was allowed to remain suspended and neither $100 nor a single cent was ever paid.[15] After he had cooled down, Bowles began to realize that he and his cause had been victorious. A close friend, joyous upon learning of the verdict, wrote: "Good enough! The victory is yours in everything but the skin of technicality. Old Phelps would sooner have taken one hundred hot burning coals on the top of his pate than that award of $100 . . . . God save the *Springfield Republican!* Bully for you Sam Bowles."[16]

Bowles became a hero with America's newspaper editors, who saw him as a champion of a free press and the *Republican* as a model of what an independent newspaper should be like. Bowles, characteristically, printed numerous favorable notices from around the country. He was, however, secure enough to also print less than flattering remarks from the editor of the *Yarmouth* (Cape Cod) *Register*: "Bowles made a great show of high toned public virtue, but everyone who knows the *Republican* knows that this is simply a cloak to hide the spite, malignity, and general cussedness of this common sewer of bile and malignity. There is not a more foul-mouthed slanderer in Massachusetts than the *Republican* and its manager, and the idea of his setting up as a champion of free discussion and an untrammeled press is perfectly ridiculous."[17]

More than anything else, Bowles needed rest that summer. He had often worked around the clock on the case, indeed, often putting in more time than his high-priced defense team. Instead of a vacation, however, he threw himself into his newspaper work with a vengeance. Times were still tough in 1875; the rival *Union* had been forced to cut wages of all its employees by ten percent.[18] Bowles was determined to put out an even better *Republican*, a newspaper that already had a reputation as one of the best in the nation.

Bowles had long been troubled by one aspect of the newspaper operation—the business office or "counting room," as it was called. Bowles thought the practices of the office were inefficient, and he made suggestions that went unheeded. The office manager was stubborn and did not appreciate the intrusion. Bowles had enough, and by letter he fired the man. This out-of-work accountant was Bowles' younger brother Frank. The terms of the dismissal were generous. Frank Bowles was told to take a year's vacation at full pay and then arrangements for the future would be discussed.[19]

Frank Bowles was crushed. He knew his brother was somewhat dissatisfied with his work, but he never expected to be fired. He had just built a fine new home on the site of his father's old home at School and Union streets and he was living there with his young family. It looked as if the whole world had caved in on him. He wandered around town with a mournful look, the deep hurt obvious to even casual acquaintances. According to the consensus in town, Samuel Bowles had done a callous thing. The stubborn owner, however, refused to comment on the matter. If he would have spoken, he would have acknowledged that Frank Bowles had integrity and a fine character, and that he was a caring father and uncle. But he did not have the knack of human relations; he often offended potential clients with his tactlessness. He would have been happier living the life of an English country gentleman.

In any event, Frank Bowles went to Europe and Egypt, and he wrote a few letters that were published in the *Republican*. The brothers exchanged letters which dealt in part with the possibility of a consulship for Frank. When that fell through, editor Bowles proposed a new line of work. Frank would write articles of a literary nature and cover special events like the impending Centennial Exposition to be held in Philadelphia. Despite the diminished responsibilities, Bowles assured Frank that his salary would not be reduced. When the letter reached Frank in the spring of 1876, he was in Paris and he was ill. Like other members of the Bowles family, Frank did not have a very rugged constitution. Later, he contracted a fever in Rome, and shortly afterwards he died. A memorial service was later held in Springfield. "Never," said a friend, "did I see Mr. Bowles look so sad as on that day."[20]

Bowles looked poorly for another reason; he was sick again. But this time something happened he could not ignore. One day in the summer of 1876, while descending stairs at the *Republican* building, he found himself sitting down, dazed, uncertain of what had happened. This must have frightened him, but he kept silent about the incident. He alluded to it only once, in a letter to Charles Allen. He described a new regimen that he embarked upon and he closed with the telling comment, "all which is to enable me to go on with my work and escape paralysis."[21]

Suffering dyspepsia that summer, Bowles left for Saratoga Springs where he met a distinguished doctor from Cincinnati, Roberts Bartholow. The doctor had a theory that impressed the ailing Bowles. His treatment involved a strict diet, with no medicine. Bowles could drink milk and only milk for a few weeks. Solid food was prohibited. Later Bartholow would let Bowles know what he could eat. Bowles told his wife that he had started the diet and expected to get "ferocious." The doctor recommended that Bowles continue to work, but the editor found it difficult as he was "powerful weak." Bowles was finally allowed to eat—in progressive steps—a cracker, an egg, broths, and then meat, fruits, and vegetables. Bowles began to feel a little stronger and he terminated the experiment.[22]

Bowles had his heart set on attending the nation's Centennial Exposition, but thought it too risky to travel such a long distance. He urged his wife and children to go. From the newspaper he sent its young assistant editor, Solomon Bulkley Griffin, who was worried that getting a hotel room might prove difficult for such a popular exhibit. Bowles told him not to worry; simply telegraph ahead and put the reservation in his name.[23]

As poorly as he felt, Bowles still managed to involve himself in the thick of the 1876 presidential campaign. He supported the Boston brahmin, Charles Francis Adams. Bowles' friend Whitelaw Reid of the *New York Tribune* also backed Adams, but it troubled Reid that Bowles supported Adams so enthusiastically that he "vulgarized" the name and actually hurt Adams' chances. Bowles proved correct when he told a friend in November of 1875 that Grant would never be renominated for a record-breaking third term.[25] Indeed, the next month, the House of Representatives, in an unprecedented action, resolved that "it would be unwise, unpatriotic, and fraught with peril" for Grant to seek another term. The resolution passed by an incredible margin of 234 to 18.[26]

The Republicans met in Cincinnati, but Bowles' poor health prevented his attendance at the convention.[27] The odds-on favorite was the charismatic Speaker of the House, the "plumed knight," James G. Blaine of Maine. As indicated, Bowles disliked Blaine for his tactics in securing the speakership over Henry Dawes. Blaine's hopes for the nomination were dashed by the taint of scandal. Critics charged that Blaine had used his position to profit from the securities of the Little Rock and Fort Smith Railroad. Realizing that Adams had little chance, as a second choice Bowles turned to the Secretary of the Treasury, Benjamin Bristow of Kentucky, a reformer who helped break the "Whiskey Ring" scandal. Much to Bowles' surprise, the convention turned to a relatively obscure candidate, Ohio Governor Rutherford B. Hayes. Called "the Great Unknown," Hayes was a solid, sober man, an honest and able administrator with mild reformist tendencies.[28] Perhaps most importantly, Hayes had no enemies. As Henry Adams put it, Hayes was "a third-rate nonentity, whose only recommendation is that he is obnoxious to no one."[29]

In late June of 1876, the Democrats met in St. Louis and nominated New York's Governor, Samuel J. Tilden. A prominent corporate lawyer, Tilden had won fame by helping to smash the notorious Tweed Ring. Tilden ran on a platform denouncing corruption and misrule under Grant. If elected, he promised civil service reform and an open and honest government.[30]

Both party platforms were mildly reform-oriented and vague. Differences remained, however, over sectional relationships. Hayes "waved the bloody shirt" and tried to reinvigorate hatred against the party which, he claimed, was responsible for the Civil War. He told audiences that a Democratic victory would cost patriots the fruits of the peace. Ironically, federal officials who were products of the spoils system, along with dedicated life-long foes of it, like Samuel Bowles, fell into line and supported Hayes. Republicans emphasized Hayes' honesty while questioning Tilden's patriotism.[31]

At *Springfield Republican* headquarters, opinion divided. Bowles supported Hayes with a moderate enthusiasm while his chief editorial writer and eldest son Samuel backed Tilden.[32] Bowles' waning energies that year were spent on two other political contests. The seventy-six year old freshman congressman, Chester Chapin, faced a tough re-election challenge. More importantly, the state Democratic Party nominated for governor none other than Charles Francis Adams. The *Republican* exulted: "Sense and statesmanship at last!"[33]

Bowles, not surprisingly, supported Chapin, who had worked

hard in Washington and served on the influential Ways and Means Committee. His voting record generally pleased Bowles, but Chapin had trouble at home, hurt by a questionable railroad transaction. Chapin headed the Boston and Albany line and also had a controlling interest in the Ware River Railroad. The latter had been leased as a branch to the Boston and Albany, thus profiting Chapin. In the making of the lease, Chapin was "on both sides of the bargain," a position Bowles regularly castigated for years. Bowles forgave Chapin, unlike the legislative committee of investigation and the voters.

Local Republicans nominated George D. Robinson to oppose Chapin. Bowles objected to Robinson on the grounds that he was hand-picked by the local machine bosses and was not sufficiently reform-minded. Bowles conceded, however, that Robinson was a "careful and . . . industrious person [with] many excellent qualities for the details of public service . . . and a prudent, cautious man, with good New England principles and habits."[34]

On Election Day, November 9, Bowles apparently struck out. The voters spurned Chapin, Adams lost badly, and Hayes seemed to have lost by a narrow margin. Tilden had garnered 4,287,000 votes and 50.9 percent of the vote to Hayes' 4,035,000, or 47.9 percent. Minor party candidates split the remaining popular vote. More importantly, Tilden had 184 electoral votes while Hayes claimed 165 with twenty votes in dispute. All Tilden needed was a single electoral vote to win. Little wonder that Tilden supporters celebrated.[35]

Republican party leaders, however, were not about to give up without a fight. Claiming fraud and intimidation of black voters in the three disputed southern states, they declared Hayes the rightful president-elect. The nation was in an uproar. Republicans stood firm while some hot-headed Democrats vowed that Hayes would not live long enough to be inaugurated. Talk of violence and revolution permeated the nation as congressmen took to wearing firearms and Grant strengthened the military garrison in Washington.[36] Both parties sent teams of observers to the contested states of Louisiana, South Carolina, and Florida. As expected, the three states submitted two sets of returns, one Democratic and one Republican, and there was an unprecedented constitutional crisis. The Constitution simply states that electoral returns from the states shall be sent to Congress and *opened* by the President of the Senate. But the major question left unanswered by the Constitution was who should *count* them? If counted by the Senate President—a Republican—the Republican returns would be validated. If counted by the Speaker of the House— a Democrat—the Democratic returns would prevail. Many agreed with Bowles' friend, editor Henry Watterson of the *Louisville Courier-Journal*, an impassioned Tilden supporter, that one hundred thousand Democratic "petitioners" should surround the Capitol while the votes were being recorded.[37] Chaos or compromise seemed the only choices. Official Washington opted for the latter. The Electoral Count Act of January, 1877, broke the stalemate. Bowles reported that the only good thing coming out of the mess was that office-seekers had not yet descended on Washington.[38]

The Act established an Electoral Commission of fifteen people— five each from the Senate, House, and Supreme Court. The commission was divided between both parties with the fifteenth man, Supreme Court Justice David Davis, presumably an Independent. At the last minute, however, Davis resigned from the bench and accepted an open Senate seat from Illinois. Justice Joseph Bradley, a New Jersey Republican, replaced him on the commission. Subsequently, by a straight party vote, the commission gave every disputed electoral vote to Hayes. Congress accepted the verdict on March 2, 1877, only two days before Inauguration Day. Since March 4 fell on a Sunday, the bearded Hayes was privately sworn into office on Saturday. Public ceremonies on March 5 went off without incident.[39]

"The Compromise of 1877" was made possible by the defection of southern Democrats who made several behind-the-scenes deals with the Republicans. The Republicans promised that, if elected, Hayes would withdraw federal troops from South Carolina and Louisiana, thus insuring the collapse of their tottering Republican state governments. Hayes' operatives also pledged federal money for southern internal improvements as well as a pledge to subsidize a transcontinental railroad along a southern route. Furthermore, Hayes' friends promised that the new postmaster-general—the most patronage-laden cabinet position—would be a southerner. In return, southern Democrats agreed to accept James Garfield as the new House Speaker. They also agreed to refrain from partisan reprisals against southern Republicans and to accept in good faith the Reconstruction amendments.[40]

In discussing the incredible circumstances that placed Hayes in the White House, Bowles urged his readers to "Look forward and not back." He added: "We live, and time goes on, and each year as it becomes the present does much to obliterate the past . . . . The Democrats must not rely on their past wrongs as their future capital. For the Republicans, this event makes a break with the past . . . . Old wounds must be suffered to heal by being let alone."[41]

Bowles vowed, however, to keep a watchful eye on the Washington scene. But he harnessed his rapidly diminishing energies on local matters. All his life he suffered physically. But there were always periods when he felt better, if not entirely well. 1877 would be different.

NOTES

1. Merriam, II:342.

2. Ibid., p. 346.

3. S.R., April 15, 1875, p. 4, col. II.

4. Ibid., April 23, 1875, p. 4, col. II.

5. Ibid., April 28, 1875, p. 4, col. VI.

6. Merriam, II:316. The Republican had been tried for libel one other time in its history and won. Lucieus Truesdeal, a hotel-keeper from Monson, filed suit against the newspaper because of a letter printed in it by Reverend Hammond, principal of Monson Academy. Hammond had described the hotel as something like "a common grogshop harmful to the morals and offensive to the public opinion of the town . . . ." See S.R., April 21, 1875, p. 4, col. II.

7. Frisch, p. 188. In 1874, Bowles protested the awarding of an honorary degree from Amherst College to Phelps' son John. Bowles, an Amherst trustee, wrote the college's president: "Had I been present when the name was suggested, I should have felt obligated to say that he was not fit for the honor of Amherst—He is a notorious liar; he is a vulgar, coarse, brutal fellow, a corrupter and a briber of voters; he has been treated by his family physician for venereal disease since he was a married man." See Bowles to (illegible), undated, Bowles Papers. That Bowles knew the latter fact is hardly surprising; he had his personal sources all over western Massachusetts.

8. S.R., April 29, 1875, p. 5, col. I.

9. Ibid., April 30, 1875, p. 5, cols. II-IV.

10. Ibid., May 1, 1875, p. 5, col. I. Dow, who apprenticed at the Republican, later founded the Wall Street Journal.

11. That statement was of dubious validity.

12. S.R., May 1, 1875, p. 4, col. VI.

13. Ibid., May 6, 1875, p. 5, col. II.

14. Merriam, II:317.

15. Hooker, p. 142, and S.R., June 13, 1875, p. 4, col. II. Bowles quickly adopted the prevailing view of the trial's outcome. As he wrote to a friend, "It was a great victory in the libel suit ... a greater one than appears on the surface. We should have had the letter of the law as well as the spirit, but the spirit was so sweeping that it killed the letter and set up the REPUBLICAN before our local public as no other incident in its history ever did." See John Hooker, Some Reminiscences of a Long Life (Hartford: Belknap and Warfield, 1899), p. 47.

16. Richard D. Hubbard to Samuel Bowles, May 6, 1875, Bowles Papers. Hubbard was elected Governor of Connecticut the next year. The Republican rationalized that Endicott awarded $100 to the seventy year old Phelps, who was in poor health, because he felt sorry for him. See S.R., May 6, 1875, p. 5, col. II.

17. S.R., May 26, 1875, p. 3, col. IV.

18. Ibid., May 27, 1875, p. 6, col. III.

19. Merriam, II:319-320.

20. Ibid., II:321. Bowles received many condolence letters expressing shock at the untimely death of his brother. See as examples, Francis Tiffany to

Bowles, May 16, 1876, and J. G. Holland to Bowles, February 6, 1876, both in Bowles Papers.

21. Merriam, II:237. Bowles was feeling so poorly with a head throbbing for ten days that he couldn't attend the funeral of William S. Robinson, "Warrington," *Republican* columnist from Boston. See Merriam, II:350.

22. Ibid., II:351-352.

23. Griffin, p. 23. There would always be a room for one of America's most prominent newspaper editors.

24. Royal Cortissoz, *The Life of Whitelaw Reid*, Vol. I (New York: Scribners, 1921), p. 337.

25. Bigelow, V:228.

28. Jones, p. 495.

27. Bowles loved political conventions and the fact that he missed them in 1876, along with the two dinner parties hosted by Murat Halstead that, Bowles wrote, "shouldn't be missed," testified to his poor physical condition. See Bowles to Halstead, June 22, 1876, Halstead Papers.

28. O'Connor, p. 267.

29. George Tindall, *America: A Narrative History* (New York: Norton, 1984), p. 702.

30. O'Connor, p. 267.

31. Jones, p. 497.

32. Bowles told an Amherst College professor that this was proof of the "independence which the *Republican* office exhibited." See Griffin, p. 160. Of course, the differences between Hayes and Tilden were not great. If Bowles' son would have supported Grant in 1872, he would have been livid.

33. Merriam, II:275.

34. Ibid., pp. 275-277. Chapin looked forward to a trip to Saratoga with Bowles after his re-election. See Chapin to Bowles, June 20, 1876, Bowles Papers.

35. *Republican* editor Griffin, a staunch Tilden man, was invited to a big victory party in New York. Apparently, Bowles would not let him go. See Griffin, p. 166 and Sidney Pomerantz, "Election of 1876" in *History of American Presidential Elections*, edited by Arthur Schlesinger, Jr., p. 1380.

36. O'Connor, p. 268. Both sides' behavior was suspect. Lew Wallace, northern politician and author of *Ben Hur*, visited Florida and Louisiana after the election and wrote, "Money and intimidation can obtain the oath of white man as well as black to any required statement . . . ." See Garraty, p. 413.

37. Bailey, p. 461, and Donald, p. 259.

38. *S.R.*, February 14, 1877, p. 4, col. I. Because he felt so poorly, Bowles did not enjoy Washington. See Bowles to Dawes, February 17, 1877, Dawes Papers.

39. O'Connor, p. 269.

40. Tindall, pp. 703-704.

41. Merriam, II:303-304.

CHAPTER X

FAREWELL

State and local politics always interested Bowles to an even greater extent than did the national arena. In 1877, he became active in the movement for reform of Springfield's government. The task of creating a new charter fell upon Probate Judge William S. Shurtleff, who chaired a committee appointed by the city government. Bowles asked Shurtleff to show him his work-in-progress, and the judge agreed. The two men held a series of discussions on the matter, and Shurtleff thanked the editor for his suggestions and criticisms.[1]

The radical new plan pleased Bowles. It reorganized Springfield's ward structure, taking into account the city's rapid growth since 1852. It provided for nine redrawn wards with a city council of nine aldermen and twenty-seven common councilmen. Addressing the problem of inefficiency and a too rapid turnover, the new plan expanded the mayor's term to two years, and called for some councilors to be elected annually, and others every two years. In addition, it strengthened the mayor's power; besides his longer term, the plan gave him additional power of appointments and more leeway in making administrative decisions. Perhaps most importantly, the charter established four consolidated administrative boards to advise the mayor and conduct the day-to-day affairs of government. The boards would oversee matters of health, fire, police, public works, and finance. Under the new charter, exclaimed the *Republican*, the public would finally have the ability to say to somebody: "Thou art the man!"[2]

The new charter plan was unveiled late that winter. Public meetings were held as interested residents vigorously discussed the pros and cons. The political establishment looked favorably upon it. Springfield's city aldermen and common councilmen, along with the state Senate, endorsed it unanimously. In the House, only one legislator voted in opposition. Only one hurdle remained, the consent of

RESIDENCE OF
SAM.L. BOWLES.

Springfield voters in a special election. Bowles and other charter boosters were confident of a big victory. Therefore, they were stunned when that spring, city voters rejected the new measure by a better than two-to-one margin.

It seems that local politicians campaigned against it, fearing a loss of power and patronage. They convinced many voters that under the new plan, the mayor would become a "king." Secondly, apparently believing an easy victory inevitable, some supporters failed to vote. Finally, in the midst of depression, many refused to give more power to those who were blamed for causing the hard times. Bowles decried the fact that there were "people who seem to find it impossible to believe that their fellow men can interest themselves in public affairs for any but base or purely personal motives."[3]

Simultaneously that winter, Bowles helped launch Springfield's Union Relief Association. Bowles volunteered for the post of chief fundraiser. He buttonholed friends, acquaintances, and even former foes and quickly tallied four thousand dollars in contributions.[4] The Union Relief functioned on various levels. It served as a clearing house for diverse governmental and private charities. It also worked unofficially to monitor and investigate the welfare system. Its first report resulted in the removal of children from almhouses and placing them in foster homes. The Union Relief also aided "street people" by replacing a previously ineffective out-door aid program.[5] Bowles used the *Republican* to promote the Association's aims. He called his paper practically "an organ of charity and prison reform."[6]

In the late spring of 1877, Bowles received an invitation from *Cincinnati Commercial* editor Murat Halstead to come for a visit. They would, Halstead wrote, spend some time in the city, but also, along with mutual friend Henry Watterson of the *Louisville Courier*, relax in the blue-grass country. Bowles hesitated, uncertain if he should go, feeling the way he did. After a great deal of thought, he decided to head west.[7]

Seeing his old comrades lifted his spirits but did little to help his faltering digestive system. Bowles became disconsolate because he could not enjoy the fine food and drink. After a few days he felt worse, with so much dyspepsia and weariness, he wrote Mary, "as to spoil the vacation of most of its pleasure." She must have been shocked when he added that he intended to stop at her home town,

Geneva, New York, for several hours on his way home, because he wanted to see it for a last time before he died.[8]

Back home in June, he wrote "Old Silver Dollar"—his affectionate nickname for Halstead—and playfully asked him if he would like to go on a trip to Paris and around the world. He mocked the hardworking Halstead for his increased capacity to shirk work, "leaving others to bear the heat and burden of the day and night." Bowles assured Halstead that he would be feeling fine as soon as he got the Kentucky milk out of his system.[9] He wrote Watterson thanking him for his "loving friendship and generous hospitality." In some ways, he added, the trip was tragic because it revealed to him clearly how little he could stand of fatigue or irregularity. He reminded him that unlike Halstead, he had no "super-abundance of physical power," so he could not squander his limited energy. He closed by regretting the missed opportunity to see Watterson's "sweet wife," but assured him he "would come again sometime."[10]

Through the summer, Bowles remained weak. He wrote Secretary of the Interior Carl Schurz that he felt "pretty feeble of body . . . but tolerably brave of soul . . . ."[11] Fearful of leaving Springfield, he did not trust himself "to another table and another bed." Adding to his woes was Mary's condition. Because of "a sick grandbaby," she "worried herself . . . into her own bed and hasn't left her room in three weeks."[12]

Concerned about the *Republican's* future, he offered a lead editorial position to Springfield native George S. Merriam, a young author who had occasionally contributed to the newspaper. Merriam replied that he had missed seeing and hearing from him since he had run off to the bluegrass country. In regard to editorial writing, Merriam believed he was not the right man, as he did not have "the light and quick touch" required. He was never happy, Merriam added, until he could get "to the bottom of the subject and work it up from A to Z." Merriam concluded by offering his services once a week as a signed columnist, but added that he did not think Bowles desired that type of contribution. Merriam guessed correctly.[13]

Samuel Bowles had changed that year. "The old air of audacity was gone," a friend recalled, "he looked languid, and as if the fight was all out of him." Another friend reflected: "It seemed to me that he especially wanted to be in peace and friendship with all his neighbors—he was tired of fighting." A staff member recalled how concerned he was in the summer of 1877, when Bowles acted too sweet and gentle, always speaking of the loveliness of the world. He longed to see some of the usual ugliness. The staffer feared that Bowles was going to die.[14]

In early September, Bowles was scheduled to present a paper at a meeting of the American Social Science Association. Bowles had been an active member of the Association, which was founded in 1865 by Boston reformers. The Association believed that government should take a positive role in dealing with social problems. Bowles vigorously supported the Association's goals, and many considered the *Republican* its unofficial organ.[15] Fortunately, the group met in Saratoga Springs, New York, less than two hundred miles from Springfield. Bowles refused to let his poor health prevent him from going. On September 7, he read his paper, "Observations on the Relations of State and Municipal Governments, and the Reform of the Latter." Bowles argued that the cities were becoming more powerful than the states. This was a dangerous trend, he believed, as the cities were becoming bastions of debt, waste, extravagance, and corruption. One solution he offered was to abolish the local police and only have state law enforcement authorities.[16]

Later that month, when his daughter, who had been away, came to see him, his appearance shocked her. He said to her, half-jokingly, "I shall have to have a valet; I can hardly brush my hair without sitting down."[17] Maria Whitney, upon her return from Europe, visited her dear friend. She too was stunned to find him "feeble to the last degree," and she thought it would take months before he would be up and about again.[18]

In October, upon a recommendation from a friend, he left for Philadelphia to consult with Dr. S. Weir Mitchell. He spent several days under his supervision, after which Mitchell urged complete rest and a strict diet. Bowles came home in worse shape, having caught a cold en route. He rested and only occasionally dictated a letter to his secretary.[19]

Halstead wrote, concerned about Bowles' condition. Bowles replied that it was true, he was confined to bed and was very sick. "It is a general debility," he informed Halstead, "nervous system used up, stomach feeling pretty entirely so, and a bronchial lung difficulty added. The last," he said, "was the feather that broke me down." Bowles concluded by assuring his friend that he intended to "pull through and do some work yet."[20]

Bowles kept up with national politics as best as he could, but his views hardened as he convalesced. To newly-elected Senator Henry Spofford, he described Washington as "rather like the top of a boil on the human system—the very center and heart of all the worst elements in the political body." He wrote Springfield Congressman George D. Robinson wishing him well. He hoped Robinson would like Washington, but added that he had always found it a trying place, and that he usually got "sick and disgusted there."[21]

In November, the *Hartford Courant's* Charles Dudley Warner made the short trip to Springfield to interview Bowles. The bedridden editor told him, with a wan smile, that nothing was wrong with him "but thirty-five years of hard work." Warner brought up the possibility of a trip to England, and Bowles expressed his doubts. Warner noted that Bowles' mind seemed as sharp as ever, but that he now viewed the world with a "philosophical calmness." A friend remembered him pale and thin, and was struck by the sight of his wife, feeding him by the mouthful, his weakness was so pronounced. He told her that he had never sought fame, that he believed work had been given him to do, and that he had only partly finished it. "Perhaps," he said, "I must leave it for other hands to finish." Leaving, she recalled his voice quivering and tears streaming down his gaunt face. Yet as late as Thanksgiving, hope remained. Bowles' daughter, Sallie Hooker, asked Dr. Smith if her family should postpone a scheduled trip to the south. Cautiously optimistic, Smith advised the Hookers to leave for the warmer climate. Despite nagging doubts, but with the doctor's assent, they left Springfield. They were not gone long.[22]

On Saturday, December 1, 1877, at one a.m., Bowles suffered a severe stroke. Two doctors came immediately, as Bowles could not speak, much of the right side of his body was paralyzed, and he had difficulty swallowing. Morphine eased his suffering. A few hours later, he partially regained his speech and said: "I guess my work is done; I think I might have done a little more but I am ready to go now." Someone asked him if he was afraid to die, and he emphatically replied "No, not at all." He bade farewell to Mary and his six children and he asked for a picture of Sallie. Pressing it to his heart, he murmured, "She understood me." Then there was a flash of the crusty editor as he said to those around him, "I am going, but not quite yet; you are in too much of a hurry."[23]

The next day Bowles' condition improved ever so slightly. A steady parade of visitors stopped by to see him, most undoubtedly thinking it was for the last time. He must have been especially grateful to see the Alexanders. The wounds of the congressional campaign still lay deep, but they could not stay away. Despite great difficulty, he had long conversations with his son Samuel about family matters, business concerns, and, of course, the *Republican*. Forty-eight hours after his stroke, the initially pessimistic doctors now voiced hope for a possible recovery.[24]

In the weeks that followed, letters of concern came by the bunchful to Bowles' Central Street home. Schuyler Colfax, ex-Vice President and Bowles' western travelling companion, wrote Mary urging her to give him Koumfys, "the Tartar-milk wine." It works wonders, he added, and had an excellent reputation in Chicago.[25] The *Chicago Tribune's* H. D. Lloyd sent a box of it to Springfield, and he noted that it worked for Senator Morton. Lloyd insisted that the medicine he sent had to be tried.[26]

Republican readers were kept up-to-date on Bowles' condition. On December 10, they were informed that Bowles was more comfortable, slept a lot, but had lost at least twenty pounds.[27] Little more than a week later, the paper reported good news; Bowles was gaining strength and had toast, eggs, and coffee for breakfast.[28] *Republican* readers learned late in the month that Bowles was struggling against congestion of the lungs, but was still eating "a considerable amount of food."[29]

Bowles found solace in the numerous visitors to his sickbed. His nurse recalled that he "watched the faces of his friends with an intense eagerness. Every nerve in [his] poor worn-out body seemed to come to the surface and clamor for help." She likened his face to "a suffering child's or a wounded animal's."[30]

The new year, 1878, found Bowles remaining in a terribly weakened condition. The *Republican* reported Bowles "exceedingly feeble,"[31] On the fourteenth, the newspaper announced that Bowles had been losing strength for several days and was quite low.[32] It seemed now only a matter of time. On January 16, at about ten p.m., Bowles suffered another paralytic stroke. Conscious to the end, with a merciful anaesthetic given to ease his agony, little over an hour later he died. On February 9, he would have been fifty-two.[33]

Bowles' obituary appeared in the *Republican* less than eight hours after his death. He would have liked that; the *Republican*, Bowles insisted, had to be as "fresh" as humanly possible. Readers were told of his "rare persistence," and his "intense devotion to his work." They were reminded of his important role in breaking down the Know-Nothing Party, and in the formation of the Republican Party. They were told about his chronic poor health which included bouts of dyspepsia, insomnia, and nervous exhaustion. His well-disciplined staff always expressed his sentiments whether he was at home or away. Bowles attended the Unitarian church but, because his work interfered with his Sundays, he could not attend on a regular basis. He was, however, a man of deep religious feeling. The obituary closed with a quote from F. B. Sanborn, that Bowles had a "genius for journalism," and was endowed with "intuitive sagacity."[34]

Bowles' death produced a profusion of editorial comment across the nation. Horace Greeley's opinion that the *Springfield Republican* was "the best and ablest country journal ever published on this continent" echoed throughout the country. Horace White of the *Chicago Tribune* wrote that Bowles symbolized "the highest aims of journalism" and that anyone who apprenticed with him "was sure of a situation in the first vacancy on any high-class journal between the oceans."[35] Dr. Holland, then with *Scribner's*, simply stated that Samuel Bowles was America's greatest newspaper editor.[36]

Bowles had earlier requested a quiet and simple funeral. Services were held in his Central Street home and only attended by those closest to him. The short ceremony included a poem read by Sanborn, singing by a male quartet, and Scripture reading by several ministers. His body was taken to Springfield Cemetery—only minutes from his home—and quietly laid to rest.[37] Several days later a Memorial Service, open to the public, took place at Springfield's Church of Unity. Men and women came from near and far in an impressive turnout. Last respects were paid by a wide assortment of prominent journalists and politicians, along with other less noteworthy area residents. Letters were read from many congressmen, ambassadors, and journalists who could not attend. Horace White, who made the long trip from Chicago, said that Bowles "was the pioneer and leader of independent journalism in the United States." Murat Halstead said that "there was in him a sweet humanity that sorrowed over all the hurts in the battle of life." Halstead added that Bowles had "the hand of a warrior; but his heart was soft—the heart of a woman." Holland testified to the purity of Bowles' life: "it was absolutely free from the stains which youthful folly and maturer vice leave upon the record of so many of our great men." Miss Brackett wrote: "Of all the men I have ever known, he was the only one who never made a woman feel as if he were condescending in thought or word when he talked to her." Others went on to praise Bowles' reform spirit, courage, and intellect. Bowles would have loved it—and he would have made sure the entire proceeding was covered in the *Republican*.[38]

Many people found it difficult to believe that Samuel Bowles had died.[39] For at least a generation his presence had loomed large in Springfield. Yet the community found solace in the fact that the new editor-in-chief would be his twenty-seven year old son Samuel.[40] The younger Bowles would carry on the tradition of his father, who had pronounced on his death-bed, "I may die but *THE REPUBLICAN* will live."[41]

NOTES

1. Merriam, II:323.

2. Frisch, p. 215.

3. Merriam, II:324 and Frisch, pp. 216-217. The voters' mindset was shaped to a large degree by *Republican* editorials that frequently emphasized the "base and purely personal motives" of men running for political office.

4. Merriam, II:326.

5. Frisch, p. 225.

6. Merriam, II:422.

7. Ibid., p. 416.

8. Ibid., p. 417.

9. Bowles to Murat Halstead, June 12, 1877, Halstead Papers.

10. Merriam, II:418-419.

11. Schurz, III:413.

12. Hooker, *Reminiscences of a Long Life*, p. 69.

13. George S. Merriam to Bowles, June 11, 1877, Bowles Papers. Merriam, Bowles' future biographer, praised the *Republican* effusively and wished he was with Bowles. If Bowles were there, he would learn from him "ever so much" he could never get out of books. See Merriam to Bowles, August 20, 1877, Bowles Papers.

14. Merriam, II:425.

15. William Leach, *True Love and Perfect Union: The Feminist Reform of Sex and Society* (New York: Basic Books, 1980), p. 298. See also Thomas Haskell, *The Emergence of Professional Social Science: The A.S.S.A. and The Nineteenth Century Crisis of Authority* (Urbana: University of Illinois Press, 1977).

16. *S.R.*, September 8, 1877, p. 8, col. I.

17. Merriam, II:427.

18. Leyda, II:281. In another letter, he told her that all she owed him was her "undying affection" which he would claim as soon as he was well enough. See Merriam, II:432.

19. Merriam, II:428.

20. Bowles to Halstead, October 23, 1877, Halstead Papers.

21. Merriam, II:430.

22. Ibid., pp. 433-434.

23. *S.R.*, December 3, 1877, p. 4, col. I, and Merriam, II:435.

24. *S.R.*, December 4, 1877, p. 4, col. I, and Merriam, II:435.

25. Schuyler Colfax to Mrs. Bowles, December 4, 1877, Bowles Papers.

26. H. D. Lloyd to Samuel Bowles, December 6, 1877, Bowles Papers.

27. *S.R.*, December 10, 1877, p. 6, col. I.

28. Ibid., December 20, 1877, p. 5, col. IV.

29. Ibid., December 29, 1877, p. 6, col. II.

30. Merriam, II:437.

31. *S.R.*, January 8, 1878, p. 6, col. IV.

32. Ibid., January 14, 1878, p. 6, col. I.

33. Merriam, II:440 and *S.R.*, January 17, 1878, p. 4, col. I. According to the *Republican* account, his last stroke was his third one.

34. *S.R.*, January 17, 1878, p. 4, col. III. Bowles, for the most part, was not a man of "deep religious feelings," as the obituary stated.

35. Hooker, p. 147, and Merriam, II:443.

36. *S.R.*, January 17, 1878, p. 5, col. II. Holland's statement was not hyperbole. After Horace Greeley's death in 1872, Bowles was considered by most to be America's best newspaper editor. *The New Haven Journal and Courier* got a little carried away, calling Bowles' *Republican* the best newspaper in the world.

37. Ibid., January 21, 1878, p. 2, col. II.

38. Merriam, II:442-446.

39. *S.R.*, March 2, 1878, p. 3, col. II.

40. Bowles' namesake was quiet, unassuming and less controversial than his father. Unlike his father, young Sam had a fine formal education. He took courses at Yale in 1871 and 1872 and a term at the University of Berlin. He also received an A.M. degree from Amherst College. See *TIME AND THE OUR*, vol. IX, No. 7, January 21, 1899. When Bowles died in 1915 at the age of sixty-four, after thirty-seven years as editor-in-chief, *The Nation* noted that he had maintained the *Republican* "at the high level upon which his father had placed in it." See *The Nation*, March 18, 1915.

41. *S.R.*, February 4, 1878. Bowles died a wealthy man. His assets were well over $100,000. He left $5,000 to Miss Slathea Easler—long-term house-

keeper—out of his life insurance. Mary received $10,000 out of life insurance and all property in the Central Street home including the horse and cow. Everything else, the rest of life insurance and interest in the *Republican* was put in trust to Charles Allen of Greenfield, his life-long friend and Massachusetts Supreme Court Justice, and to his son Samuel for payment of debts, maintenance of the family home for his wife and children, and for final distribution among heirs. Bowles owned property on Adams Street, Main Street, Lombard Street, Pearl Street, and Maynard Farms on Boston Road in Springfield. See Hampden County Probate Court, Estate of Samuel Bowles, Hampden County Courthouse, Springfield.

EPILOGUE

I spent six years living with Samuel Bowles. He was difficult to escape from, even on weekends. The Bowles name looms large in Springfield. My in-laws, Thomas and Beatrice Eastwood, live only a few hundred yards from the Samuel Bowles school. Shopping downtown on Saturdays, I often passed the Bowles building. About the first thing I would do on Sunday mornings, would be to pick up the *Springfield Republican* from the front stoop!

How do I feel about Samuel Bowles? Mixed feelings, I confess. Certainly there is much to admire about the man and his achievements. Practically single-handedly, he turned the *Springfield Republican* into one of the nation's best newspapers and probably the premier paper published outside of a large city. His perseverance, dedication, and zeal were unmatched by rival editors. He was way ahead of his time in his call for women's suffrage. His concern for the less fortunate, especially in his later years, was genuine. His dedication in exposing political corruption at all levels of government was often commendable. Bolting from the Republican Party in 1872 cost him friends and circulation losses, yet he stood firm. His travel books vividly sketched the physical features and cultures of the American West, enthralling tens of thousands of readers. Bowles' achievements are made more striking when his chronic poor health is taken into consideration. Three breakdowns—the first at age nineteen—dyspepsia, bowel difficulties, sciatica, severe headaches (probably migraine), frequent lung problems, and other ailments dogged him throughout his life.

On the other hand, Bowles had his dark side. Vainglorious, hypocritical, selfish, stubborn, and vindictive, he was also occasionally cowardly in his dealings with family and friends. Bowles liked to boast that he and his newspaper were "independent." Indeed, Richard Hooker's history of the *Republican* is entitled *The Story of an Independent Newspaper*. Yet how politically independent was Bowles and his paper when it supported Republican Party candidates

142

nineteen out of twenty times? The man who pledged that neither he nor his reporters would accept free passes from the railroads,[1] accepted a free vacation to Europe from railroad mogul Chester Chapin. Upon their return, Bowles supported Democrat Chapin for a congressional seat over his brother-in-law, Republican Henry Alexander, who, Bowles claimed, was a tool of the local political bosses. Bowles, however, never documented his charges. If Alexander's nomination was engineered by local political "bosses," then they were the same people who supported Bowles' long-time friend and confidant Henry Dawes. Bowles was an ardent foe of the spoils system and the evils of political patronage. His "holier than thou" pontifications on the subject splashed across many an editorial page column. Yet at the same time, he saw no problem at all in seeking favors from politicians for his own friends or relatives. In 1861, he wrote Dawes about an opening at the Huntington Post Office. Bowles recommended his twenty-three year old second cousin, Edward Bowles.[2] Several years later, he wrote directly to Secretary of the Navy, Gideon Welles, seeking a position for his friend, James M. Smith.[3]

Bowles' views on racial, ethnic, and religious matters were hardly enlightened. He pandered to the popular prejudices of his day. The Indians stood in the way of progress, Bowles believed, so they had to be pushed aside. Extermination, he thought, was a regretable but tolerable solution to the problem. He had little sympathy for those who practiced any religion other than his own type of Unitarian Protestantism. Mexican, Panamanian, and Chinese culture, among others, were denigrated for being different than that of New England.

Bowles' work consumed his life. He spent little time with his family. Only Sallie and Samuel—the two eldest of his seven children—seemed to win much time from him. The children undoubtedly both loved and feared their famous father. Bowles' dismissal of his brother Benjamin by letter obviously indicated a lack of courage. He showed little concern for the feelings of long-time friend and business associate Clark Bryan when he arbitrarily announced that Samuel Bowles and Company had to be dissolved.

But in the final analysis, what Bowles will be remembered for is his newspaper. His achievement was unprecedented in nineteenth-century America. The *Springfield Republican* was a model of a readable, quality newspaper. He put his heart and soul into it, and it killed him at a relatively young fifty-two. Given good health and a long life, Bowles would have played a significant role in American political culture in the remaining years of the century, perhaps even replacing Greeley as the number one editor of his era.

NOTES

1. Griffin, p. 56.

2. Bowles to Dawes, July 6, 1861, Dawes Papers. In 1869, Bowles wrote Dawes indicating he wanted "Traps" for the Wilbraham Post Office. See Bowles to Dawes, March 23, 1869, Dawes Papers.

3. Bowles to Gideon Welles, December 7, 1865, Dawes Papers.

BIBLIOGRAPHY

BOOKS

Bailey, Thomas. *The American Pageant.* Lexington, Massachusetts: D. C. Heath, 1983.

Baltzell, Edward Digby. *Puritan Boston and Quaker Philadelphia.* Boston: Beacon Press, 1979.

Bauer, Frank. *At the Crossroads: Springfield, Massachusetts 1636-1975.* Springfield: Bicentennial Committee of Springfield, 1975.

Baum, Dale. *The Civil War Party System: The Case of Massachusetts 1848-1876.* Chapel Hill: University of North Carolina Press, 1984.

Beale, Howard K., Ed. *Diary of Gideon Wells.* Vol. III. New York: Norton, 1960.

Bennet, Whitman. *Whittier, Bard of Freedom.* Chapel Hill: University of North Carolina Press, 1941.

Bianchi, Martha Dickinson. *Emily Dickinson, Face to Face.* Boston: Houghton Mifflin, 1932.

Bigelow, John. *Retrospections on an Active Life.* Vol. V. Garden City: Doubleday, 1913.

Bleyer, Williard. *Main Currents in the History of American Journalism.* Boston: Houghton Mifflin, 1927.

Bowles, Samuel. *Across the Continent: A Summer's Journey to the Rocky Mountains, The Mormons, and the Pacific States.* Springfield, Massachusetts: Samuel Bowles and Company, 1865.

————. *Our New West: Records of Travel Between the Mississippi and the Pacific Ocean.* Hartford, Connecticut: Hartford Publishing Company, 1869.

————. *The Switzerland of America: Colorado, Its Parks and Mountains.* Springfield, Massachusetts: Samuel Bowles and Company, 1868.

Brock, William. *Conflict and Transformation: The United States 1844-1877.* New York: Penguin Books, 1973.

145

Burns, James MacGregor. *The Vineyard of Liberty*. New York: Vintage, 1983.

Chester, Giraud. *Embattled Maiden: The Life of Anna Dickinson*. New York: Putnam, 1951.

Congdon, Charles T. *Reminiscences of a Journalist*. Boston: James R. Osgood and Company, 1880.

Corngold, Ralph. *Two Friends of Man*. Boston: Little, Brown, and Company, 1950.

Cortissoz, Royal. *The Life of Whitelaw Reid*. Vol. I. New York: Scribners, 1921.

Current, Richard. *Lincoln and The First Shot*. Philadelphia: Lippincott, 1963.

Donald, David. *Charles Sumner and the Coming of the Civil War*. New York: Knopf, 1960.

Fehrenbacher, Don E. *The Dred Scott Case*. New York: Oxford University Press, 1978.

Foner, Eric. *Free Soil, Free Labor, Free Men*. New York: Oxford University Press, 1970.

Frisch, Michael. *Town Into City: Springfield, Massachusetts and the Meaning of Community, 1840-1880*. Cambridge: Harvard University Press, 1972.

Green, Mason. *Springfield, 1636-1886*. Springfield: C. A. Nichols, 1888.

Griffin, Solomon Bulkley. *People and Politics Observed by a Massachusetts Editor*. Boston: Little, Brown, and Company, 1923.

Hamilton, Holman. *Prologue to Conflict: The Crisis and Compromise of 1850*. New York: W. W. Norton, 1964.

Haskell, Thomas. *The Emergence of Professional Social Science: The A.S.S.A. and The Nineteenth Century Crisis of Authority*. Urbana: University of Illinois Press, 1971.

Holliday, J. S. *The World Rushed In: The California Gold Rush Experience*. New York: Simon and Schuster, Touchstone Edition, 1983.

Hooker, John. *Some Reminiscences of a Long Life*. Hartford: Belknap and Warfield, 1899.

Hooker, Richard. *The Story of an Independent Newspaper*. New York: Macmillan, 1924.

Hudson, Frederick. *History of Journalism*. New York: Harper Brothers, 1873.

Isely, Jeter Allen. *Horace Greeley and the Republican Party*. Princeton: Princeton University Press, 1947.

James, Edward, Ed. *Notable American Women*. Vol. I. Cambridge: Belknap Press of Harvard University Press, 1971.

Johannsen, Robert. *Stephen A. Douglas*. New York: Oxford University Press, 1973.

Leach, William. *True Love and Perfect Union: The Feminist Reform of Sex and Society*. New York: Basic Books, 1980.

Leyda, Jay. *The Years and Hours of Emily Dickinson*. Two Volumes. New Haven: Yale University Press, 1960.

Longsworth, Polly. *Emily Dickinson: Her Letter to the World*. New York: Thomas Crowell, 1965.

Lucid, Richard, Ed. *The Journal of Richard Henry Dana, Jr.* Vol. II. Cambridge: Belknap Press of Harvard University Press, 1968.

Martin, Wendy. *An American Triptych: Anne Bradstreet, Emily Dickinson, Adrienne Rich*. Chapel Hill: University of North Carolina Press, 1984.

McFeely, William. *Grant: A Biography*. New York: Norton, 1981.

McHenry, Robert, Ed. *Liberty's Women*. Springfield: Merriam-Webster, 1976.

McJimsey, George T. *Genteel Partisan: Manton Marble 1834-1917*. Ames: Iowa State University Press, 1971.

Merk, Frederick. *Manifest Destiny and Mission in American History*. New York: Knopf, 1963.

Merriam, George S. *The Life and Times of Samuel Bowles*. Two Volumes. New York: The Century Company, 1885.

Miller, John C. *The Federalist Era*. New York: Harper and Row, 1960.

Miller, Ruth. *The Poetry of Emily Dickinson*. Middletown, Connecticut: Wesleyan University Press, 1968.

Nevins, Allen. *Fremont, Pathmaker of the West*. New York: D. Appleton-Century, 1939.

———. *The Emergence of Lincoln: Prologue to Civil War 1859-1861*. Vol. II. New York: Scribners, 1950.

Nichols, Roy. *The Stakes of Power*. New York: Hill and Wang, 1961.

147

Oates, Stephen B. *Abraham Lincoln: The Man Behind the Myths.* New York: Harper and Row, 1984.

———. *To Purge This Land With Blood: A Biography of John Brown.* New York: Harper and Row, 1970.

O'Connor, Thomas. *The Disunited States: The Era of Civil War and Reconstruction.* Second Edition. New York: Harper and Row, 1978.

Pease, Jane and William. *The Fugitive Slave Law and Anthony Burns: A Problem in Law Enforcement.* New York: Crowell, 1975.

Potter, David. *Division and the Stresses of Reunion.* Glenview, Illinois: Scott, Foresman, 1973.

Richards, Leonard. *Gentlemen of Property and Standing: Anti-Abolitionist Mobs in America.* New York: Oxford University Press, 1970.

Rideing, William H. *Many Celebrities and a Few Others.* Garden City, New York: Doubleday, Page, and Company, 1912.

Robinson, Mrs. William S. *Warrington Pen Portraits: A Collection of Personal and Political Reminiscences From 1848-1876.* Boston: Lee and Shepard, 1877.

Roper, Laura Wood. *F.L.O.: A Biography of Frederick Law Olmstead.* Baltimore: Johns Hopkins University Press, 1973.

Rossbach, Jeffrey. *Ambivalent Conspirators: John Brown, The Secret Six and A Theory of Slave Violence.* Philadelphia: The University of Pennsylvania Press, 1984.

Salsbury, Stephen. *The State, The Investor, and The Railroad: The Boston & Albany 1825-1867.* Cambridge: Harvard University Press, 1967.

Sanborn, Alvan F., Ed. *Reminiscences of Richard Lather.* Grafton Press, 1908.

Schlesinger, Arthur M. Jr., Ed. *History of American Presidential Elections.* Vol. II. New York: Chelsea House, 1971.

Schudson, Michael. *Discovering the News: A Social History of American Newspapers.* New York: Basic Books, 1978.

Schurz, Carl. *Speeches, Correspondence, Political Papers.* Vol. II. New York: Putnam and Sons, 1913.

Sewall, Richard. *The Life of Emily Dickinson.* New York: Farrar, Straus, and Giroux, 1974.

Singletary, Otis. *The Mexican War*. Chicago: University of Chicago Press, 1960.

Stegner, Wallace. *Beyond the Hundredth Meridian: John Wesley Powell and the Second Opening of the West*. Boston: Houghton Mifflin, 1954.

Terrel, John Upton. *The Man Who Rediscovered America: A Biography of John Wesley Powell*. New York: Weybright and Talley, 1969.

Thomas, John. *The Liberator*. Boston: Little, Brown, and Company, 1963.

Tindall, George. *America: A Narrative History*. New York: Norton, 1984.

ARTICLES

Anonymous. Review of Merriam's *The Life and Times of Samuel Bowles* in *The London Spectator* (July 24, 1886).

———— *Time and the Our*. Vol. IX (January 21, 1899).

Arcanti, Steven J. "To Secure the Party: Henry L. Dawes and the Politics of Reconstruction." *Historical Journal of Western Massachusetts* (Spring, 1977).

Downer, Matthew. "Horace Greeley and the Politicians: The Liberal Republican Convention in 1872." *Journal of American History* (March 1967).

Gladden, Washington. Review of Merriam's *The Life and Times of Samuel Bowles* in *Dial* (February 1886).

Harrison, Theresa. "George Thompson and the 1851 'Anti-Abolition' Riot." *Historical Journal of Western Massachusetts* (Spring, 1976).

Morin, Edward. "Springfield During the Civil War Years, 1861-1865." *Historical Journal of Western Massachusetts* (Fall, 1974).

Mulkern, John. "Western Massachusetts in the Know-Nothing Years: An Analysis of Voting Patterns." *Historical Journal of Western Massachusetts* (January 1980).

Prescott, G. B. "The U.S. Armory at Springfield." *Atlantic Monthly* (October 1863).

Whitney, Henry M. Review of Merriam's *The Life and Times of Samuel Bowles* in *New Englander and Yale Review* (February 1886).

NEWSPAPERS

Chicago *Times*.

New York *Herald*.

New York *Tribune*.

New York *World*.

Northampton *Courier*.

Springfield *Republican*.

Springfield *Union*.

MANUSCRIPT COLLECTIONS CONSULTED

John A. Andrew Collection. Massachusetts Historical Society, Boston.

Nathan Appleton Collection. William R. Perkins Library, Duke University. Durham, North Carolina.

Edward Atkinson Collection. Massachusetts Historical Society. Boston.

Nathaniel Prentiss Banks Collection. William R. Perkins Library. Duke University. Durham, North Carolina.

Newton Bateman Collection. Illinois State Library. Springfield, Illinois.

Samuel Bowles Collection. Yale University. New Haven, Connecticut.

Benjamin Bristow Collection. Library of Congress. Washington, DC.

William Claflin Collection. Rutherford B. Hayes Presidential Center. Fremont, Ohio.

Schuyler Colfax Collection. Indiana State Library. Indianapolis, Indiana.

Richard H. Dana Jr. Collection. Massachusetts Historical Society, Boston.

Henry L. Dawes Collection. Library of Congress. Washington, DC.

Anna Dickinson Collection. Library of Congress. Washington, DC.

Murat Halstead Collection. Cincinnati Historical Society. Cincinnati, Ohio.

Adams Sherman Hill Collection. William R. Perkins Library. Duke University. Durham, North Carolina.

Samuel May Collection. Boston Public Library. Boston, Massachusetts.

Frederick Law Olmstead Collection. Library of Congress. Washington, DC.

Whitelaw Reid Collection. Library of Congress. Washington, DC.

Carl Schurz Collection. Library of Congress. Washington, DC.

John Warner Collection. American Philosophical Society. Philadelphia, Pennsylvania.

William D. Whitney Collection. Yale University. New Haven, Connecticut.

PAMPHLET

Bowles, Samuel. *The Lawyer and His Clients: The Rights and Duties of Lawyers: The Rights and Duties of the Press: The Opinions of the Public.* Springfield: Samuel Bowles and Company, 1871.

UNPUBLISHED WORKS

Leal, Patricia. "Springfield: Meeting the Challenge of the Civil War." Submitted for History 290 C, May 8, 1975. Local History Room. Springfield Central Library. Springfield, Massachusetts.

Mitchell, John. *Springfield, Massachusetts and the Coming of the Civil War.* Ph.D. dissertation. Boston University, 1960.

Ryan, Elizabeth. "Samuel Bowles: Pioneer in Independent Journalism." Mount Holyoke College Honors Paper, 1936.

Whittlesey, Derwent S. *The Springfield Armory.* Ph.D. dissertation. University of Chicago, 1920.

INDEX

Abolition Movement, 17-18
Acapulco, Mexico, 59
Adams, Charles Francis, 22, 93-95, 122-124
Adams, Henry, 123
Adams, John, 1
Adams, John Quincy, 4
African Church, 18, 26
Alexander, Amelia, 19, 112
Alexander, Henry, 109, 111-112
Allen, Charles, 37-38, 59, 87, 118, 121, 141n
American Social Science Association, 134
Amesbury, 37
Amherst, 21, 39, 86
Amherst College, 9-10, 39, 66, 77n, 127n
Andrew, John A., 78n
Anthony, Susan B., 85
Ashmun, George, 10, 16, 27
Athol and Enfield Railroad, 106

Banks, Nathaniel, 27
Bartholow, Roberts, 122
Beach, E. D., 22
Berkshire County, 111
Berkshire Courier, 36
Berlin, University of, 140n
Blaine, James G., 103-104, 122-123
Bliss, George Jr., 2
Bond, William, 71
Boston, 6, 22, 117
Boston Atlas, 21, 38
Boston Telegraph and Chronicle, 38
Boston Traveller, 38-39
Boston and Chicago Gold Mining Company, 64n
Boutwell, George, 22, 103
Bowles, Benjamin, 43, 48, 97

Bowles, Charles Allen, 81
Bowles, Frank, 121
Bowles, John, 1
Bowles, Julia, 2
Bowles, Mary, 40, 46, 61n, 81-83, 141n; health of, 80, 133; illus., 83
Bowles, Sally, 68, 81, 117, 135
Bowles, Samuel, attitude towards Indians, 54, 70; childhood of, 5; editorial philosophy of, 36; education of, 5; estate of, 140-141n; health of, 7-8, 19, 39, 64n, 67, 114n, 121-122, 132-140; illus. of, 41, 52; marriage of, 11; position in Boston for, 38-39; travels of, 48-58, 108-109
Bowles, Samuel III, 81, 138, 140-141n
Bowles, Samuel Sr., 1-6; death of, 19
Brackett, Miss, 138
Bradley, Joseph, 125
Brattleboro, Vermont, 71
Breckenridge, John C., 27
Brevoort House, 43
Brooklyn, 19
Brooks, Preston, 23
Bross, William, 51-53, 68
Brown, B. Gratz, 92-94
Brown, John, 25-26, 30-31n
Bryan, Clark W., 36-38, 97-98
Buchanan, James, 23
Bullock, Alexander, 73
Burns, Anthony, 20
Butler, Andrew P., 23
Butler, Benjamin, 103

Calhoun, William B., 10, 66
California, 11, 55-56, 58
Cass, Lewis, 15
Chapin, Chester, 2, 106, 108-109, 111, 123-124